Cambridge Elements

Elements in Child Development
edited by
Marc H. Bornstein
National Institute of Child Health and Human Development, Bethesda
Institute for Fiscal Studies, London
UNICEF, New York City

THEORY OF MIND IN CHILDHOOD

Diane Poulin-Dubois
Concordia University

Shaftesbury Road, Cambridge CB2 8EA, United Kingdom

One Liberty Plaza, 20th Floor, New York, NY 10006, USA

477 Williamstown Road, Port Melbourne, VIC 3207, Australia

314–321, 3rd Floor, Plot 3, Splendor Forum, Jasola District Centre, New Delhi – 110025, India

103 Penang Road, #05–06/07, Visioncrest Commercial, Singapore 238467

Cambridge University Press is part of Cambridge University Press & Assessment, a department of the University of Cambridge.

We share the University's mission to contribute to society through the pursuit of education, learning and research at the highest international levels of excellence.

www.cambridge.org
Information on this title: www.cambridge.org/9781009598736

DOI: 10.1017/9781009413503

© Diane Poulin-Dubois 2025

This publication is in copyright. Subject to statutory exception and to the provisions of relevant collective licensing agreements, no reproduction of any part may take place without the written permission of Cambridge University Press & Assessment.

When citing this work, please include a reference to the DOI 10.1017/9781009413503

First published 2025

A catalogue record for this publication is available from the British Library

ISBN 978-1-009-59873-6 Hardback
ISBN 978-1-009-41348-0 Paperback
ISSN 2632-9948 (online)
ISSN 2632-993X (print)

Cambridge University Press & Assessment has no responsibility for the persistence or accuracy of URLs for external or third-party internet websites referred to in this publication and does not guarantee that any content on such websites is, or will remain, accurate or appropriate.

For EU product safety concerns, contact us at Calle de José Abascal, 56, 1°, 28003 Madrid, Spain, or email eugpsr@cambridge.org

Theory of Mind in Childhood

Elements in Child Development

DOI: 10.1017/9781009413503
First published online: October 2025

Diane Poulin-Dubois
Concordia University

Author for correspondence: Diane Poulin-Dubois,
diane.poulindubois@concordia.ca

Abstract: This Element describes the development of a Theory of Mind, or mentalizing, in infancy and early childhood. Theory of Mind is a key social cognitive ability that permits children to predict and explain human behaviors by attributing mental states to other people. Understanding mental states gradually progresses from basic desires to false beliefs. The Element reviews the proximal and distal cognitive and social determinants that facilitate early Theory of Mind development. Discoveries in neuroscience contribute to understanding the ontogeny of Theory of Mind. This Element presents an overview of the main theoretical accounts of Theory of Mind development and offers suggestions for future research.

This Element also has a video abstract:
www.Cambridge.org/EICD-Dubois_abstract

Keywords: theory of mind, cognition, mentalizing, infancy, childhood

© Diane Poulin-Dubois 2025

ISBNs: 9781009598736 (HB), 9781009413480 (PB), 9781009413503 (OC)
ISSNs: 2632-9948 (online), 2632-993X (print)

Contents

1 Introduction — 1

2 Do Infants Have a Theory of Mind? — 5

3 Correlates of Theory of Mind — 16

4 Theoretical Accounts of Theory of Mind Development — 32

5 Neural Foundations of Theory of Mind Development — 37

6 Summary and Future Directions — 40

7 Conclusions — 43

References — 46

1 Introduction

Humans constantly interact with other people and are considered among the most social species (Gariepy et al., 2014). They not only live socially but think socially and spontaneously explain and predict other people's behaviors. They possess a Theory of Mind (ToM), which is a sophisticated cognitive ability that concerns the attribution to others of a wide range of mental states, including intentions, desires, knowledge, true and false beliefs, and emotions (Wellman, 2014). Sometimes called intuitive psychology, naïve or folk psychology, mentalizing, or mindreading, ToM is a foundational social cognitive ability. Understanding that others have mental states different from one's own makes it possible to infer what others are thinking and to predict their behavior. ToM has roots in philosophy, particularly in the groundwork for a science of the mind laid down by the philosopher René Descartes. In psychology, the first scholar to study this cognitive ability was Jean Piaget, who suggested that before the age of 3 or 4 years egocentrism prevents children from understanding that other people's thoughts and viewpoints may differ from their own (Piaget & Inhelder, 1967). But the modern impetus for ToM came from Flavell's (1968) work on "perceptual role taking" – the ability to take another's visual perspectives – and "conceptual role taking" – the ability to take another's mental perspective, to impute another's knowledge or intentions. Similarly, Selman (1971) explored the development of conceptual role-taking and reported that conceptual role-taking is an age-related, developing social-cognitive skill.

Premack and Woodruff (1978) had coined the term ToM as it is now used in developmental science. They argued that chimpanzees and perhaps other non-human primates could understand intentions, suggesting that chimpanzees possessed a ToM. Although the depth of nonhuman primates' Theory of Mind remains controversial, Premack and Woodruff's work inspired psychologists to document Theory of Mind development in typical and atypical populations. An edited book of papers from talks presented at two conferences (Astington et al., 1988) followed by three other books (Astington, 1994; Perner, 1991; Wellman, 1990) launched a widespread interest in ToM. To fully understand any aspect of cognitive development requires documenting its origins and change. So, over the years, research on ToM has expanded in both depth and breadth (for a history of ToM research, see Wellman, 2017).

Wimmer and Perner (1983) documented the development of metarepresentation (e.g., a belief about someone's belief) with a false belief task. In the standard version of this test, a puppet named Maxi puts a chocolate in a cupboard and leaves the scene. The experimenter moves the chocolate to a new location and asks the child where Maxi will look for it. In another version

Figure 1 A depiction of the Sally-Anne task of false belief reasoning developed by Wimmer and Perner (1983). Figure reproduced from Birch et al. (2017) with permission.

called the "Sally-Anne" task, Sally and Anne put a marble in a box. Sally leaves, and Anne takes the marble out of the original box and puts it in a different box (see Figure 1). Up until about the age of 4, most children ascribe their own beliefs to Maxi and Sally and tell the experimenter that Maxi or Sally will look for the chocolate or marble in its new location. However, older children understand that Maxi will look for the chocolate where he last saw it in the cupboard, and Sally will look in the first box. The task requires that children understand that other people's beliefs may differ from their own and then predict how those people will react based on their differing beliefs.

Since the landmark paper by Wimmer and Perner, ToM has become among the most studied topics in cognitive developmental science, with numerous books and thousands of research articles published on the subject. We now have a good grasp on this foundational cognitive ability and its development from research across many disciplines. The main contributions of developmental scientists have been to document when ToM develops and the factors that account for developmental changes in understanding a range of mental states. For example, the impact of ToM development on the development of language and other social cognitive skills, such as executive functions, has been documented (Wade et al., 2018). Comparative psychologists have examined which mental states are uniquely understood by humans and which are also understood by other species (Krupenye & Call, 2019). Clinicians studying autism and other developmental disorders have also examined ToM impairments (Senju, 2012). Finally, neuroscientists have investigated if there is a distinct and domain-specific neural system for thinking about the mind (Mahy et al., 2014).

This Element on Theory of Mind is focused on the developmental period from infancy to the preschool years and aims to provide answers to four key questions about early ToM development: *What? When? Why?* and *How?* What are the typical steps in the development of ToM from infancy to age 5? What external and internal factors to the child influence the rate of ToM development? What are the consequences of Theory of Mind development for children's social competence and academic achievement? When does ToM emerge? Why is it important to study ToM? And how does ToM develop? To answer these questions, I first review milestones in the development of ToM and factors that contribute to its emergence. Then, I discuss the state of science about the emergence of an automatic, nonverbal, implicit form of ToM in human infants as well as research on the neurological correlates of ToM. I conclude with suggestions for future research in this exciting area of developmental science.

The original focus on false belief reasoning, a key milestone in early ToM, was followed by research on the multiple steps leading to that sophisticated ability. The emergence of pretend play during the second year of life is one of the first pieces of evidence that children are aware of the difference between what the mind represents and the world outside the mind (Leslie, 1987). For example, when pretending that a stick is a phone, children show that they can distinguish between an object – the stick – and thoughts about the object – the stick as a phone (Kavanaugh, 2006). By 18 months of age, they also understand that people will display happiness when their desires are fulfilled and sadness if their desires are not fulfilled (Chiarella & Poulin-Dubois, 2013; Wellman & Banerjee, 1991). During the second year, children begin to grasp that there may be a difference between what they want and what another person wants (Meltzoff et al., 1999). Such awareness is reflected in children's language as toddlers talk about what they and others want, like, and feel; when they are 3, they also talk about what other people think and know (Bartsch & Wellman, 1995).

As such, ToM develops gradually as a function of the complexity of mental states (e.g., from simple desires to false belief). Wellman and Liu (2004) documented the gradual development of ToM by developing a step-like scale that reflects a fixed sequence in understanding mental states: diverse desires, diverse beliefs, knowledge access, false beliefs, and hidden emotion (see Figure 2). Each step was assessed with a simple scenario about a character (a human figurine), using props such as boxes and drawings of scenes, and questions asked during warm-up, test, and control phases. In several converging studies conducted worldwide with adaptations in multiple languages, a typical order of difficulty has been reported, with diverse desires being the easiest and understanding hidden emotions being the hardest to understand/produce (Wellman et al., 2006, 2011; Wellman et al., 2008). This ToM scale has also been validated longitudinally by testing the same children between the ages of 3 and 6 years (Wellman et al., 2011). Children also develop metacognitive skills

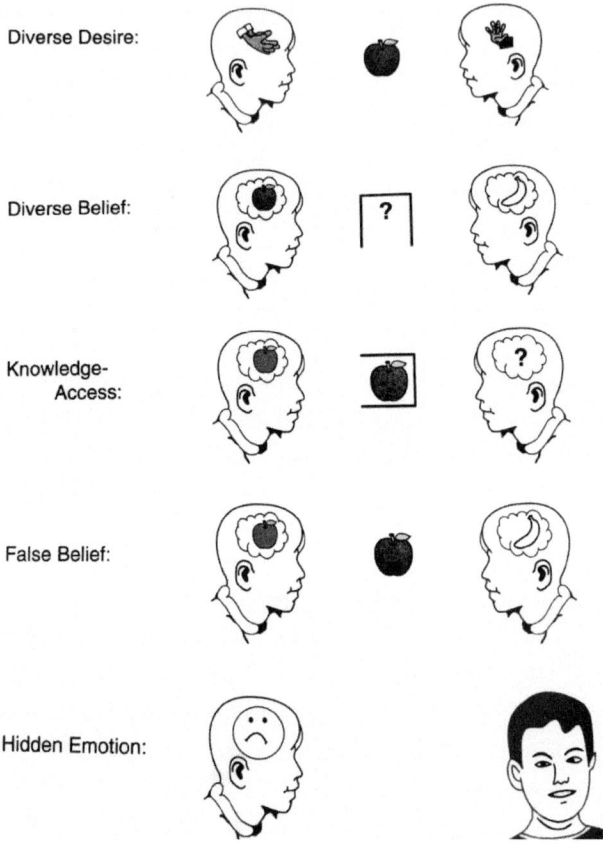

Figure 2 Wellman and Liu scale (2004). Figure reproduced from Wellman (2014) with permission.

about the mind during that same developmental period. Bialecka and her colleagues (2024) developed a measure of children's knowledge about the mind and thinking processes between the ages of 3 and 7 years. Children initially grasp that mental states do not possess physical attributes; that is, children understand that we do not have visual, auditory, or tactile access to thoughts. This knowledge is typically achieved by most 4-year-olds. Subsequently, children become aware of the internal localization of thoughts. The third milestone concerns the source of thoughts, with approximately half of 6-year-olds achieving such understanding. The final step in this developmental sequence involves the ability to define thoughts and the thinking process.

Nonetheless, some variations have been observed in the progression of these steps as a function of sociocultural differences (Peterson & Slaughter, 2017; Slaughter & Perez-Zapata, 2014). For example, both Chinese and Iranian children develop an understanding of knowledge access before any understanding of belief (Shahaeian et al., 2011; Wellman et al., 2006). In the section on the impact of culture on ToM development, I discuss underlying mechanisms that might explain this deviation from the sequence observed in most linguistic and cultural groups. Finally, there are delays in addition to deviations to the scale in certain populations, such as among deaf children born to hearing parents or children with autism. For example, deaf children progress through the steps in the same sequence, but it takes them many years to progress through the scale in comparison to hearing children (Peterson et al., 2005; Peterson & Wellman, 2009; Remmel & Peters, 2008). In contrast, children with autism deviate from the typical sequence by passing hidden emotions before false beliefs (Peterson et al., 2012). Neurotypical children vary in their ability to reason about others' mind, and these individual differences are stable over time and across tasks (Hughes & Devine, 2015).

Understanding false belief progresses beyond the forms typically mastered during the preschool years. A more advanced development is second-order false belief: the realization that it is possible to hold a false belief about someone else's belief, also called recursive mentalistic reasoning (Miller, 2009, 2012). To illustrate how first- and second-order false beliefs differ, consider Wimmer and Perner's (1983) Maxi scenario. The target for the belief could be the person who moved the chocolate in Maxi's absence, and the question is where this person thinks that Maxi thinks the chocolate is. The attribution of such a belief constitutes second-order reasoning: "A thinks that B believes ... ." By age 6, children pass second-order false belief tests (Miller, 2009). What new developments are made possible by the mastery of second-order belief? A number of social and cognitive consequences have been documented (lies, jokes, irony, etc.) (see Miller, 2009).

2 Do Infants Have a Theory of Mind?

All children's cognitive abilities (e.g., memory, categorization) are developmental achievements that have precursors. Theory of Mind is no exception. However, the question is how rich the ToM that emerges during infancy is. As pointed out earlier, Leslie (1987) proposed that the first manifestation of a capacity for metarepresentation emerges during the second year of life with pretend play. Since then, researchers have documented what specific mental states (e.g., desire, intention, belief) are understood in infancy. For some researchers, who adopt a rich, mentalistic view of early ToM, the time lag until success on standard ToM tasks can be accounted for by the complexity of the inferential process required to attribute mental states that differ from one's own as well as by the heavy cognitive load involved in standard tasks. For others, who hold a minimalist account, attribution of mental states is beyond infants' abilities.

2.1 Goals, Intentions, and Desires

In line with a rich nativist account, evidence that ToM might be mastered before children can answer questions in procedures such as the Sally and Anne task was published by Clements and Perner (1994). They recorded children's anticipatory looking before the agent returned to the scene in the change-of-location task. Children as young as 2.5 years of age correctly looked at the original location of the object but responded verbally incorrectly, stating that the protagonist would search in the new location. This result suggested that core "mind-reading" abilities might be innate or develop very early. Poulin-Dubois (1999; Poulin-Dubois & Tilden, 1996) and her colleagues first used the preferential looking paradigm to test 18-month-olds' understanding of goals by showing them video clips of an actor reaching for one of two objects repeatedly, followed by two still frames showing the actor holding one or the other object. Infants looked longer at the event reflecting a novel goal (holding the other object) than at the one reflecting the old goal (holding the same object). Woodward (1998) addressed goal understanding in even younger infants with a design based on the habituation-dishabituation paradigm. Six- and 9-month-old infants first watched a hand approach and grasp one of two objects and remain in this position until the end of the trial. Once infants had habituated (i.e., their looking time to the event decreased to a criterion), the locations of the objects were switched, and the hand reached either toward the same object in a new location (old goal) or to a previously untouched object in the familiar location (new goal). Infants dishabituated (their looking time to the event increased above criterion) to the new goal trial. When a claw replaced the human agent in a control condition, the infants failed to look above the criterion unless the claw was shown to be controlled by a person.

Evidence for some understanding of other basic ToM constructs was building around the same time, including evidence that infants are sensitive to the subjectivity of desires, that is, that one's desires can be different from those of others, by the middle of the second year with a study by Repacholi and Gopnik (1997; the so-called "broccoli experiment"). Children were offered snacks that triggered positive (crackers) and negative (broccoli) preferences. Then, an adult expressed the same preference (match) or the opposite preference (mismatch) and asked the child for a snack. Infants aged 18 months (but not 14 months) gave the adult the snack that she preferred in each condition, showing an understanding of desires as subjective (see also Egyed et al., 2013). Meltzoff (1995) showed that a grasp of intentions emerged around the same age in a study which used the re-enactment of intended actions. This procedure first involved demonstration of failed attempts or unfulfilled intentions (e.g., trying unsuccessfully to pull a toy dumbbell apart) followed by the child's imitation, who tended to complete the actions successfully, suggesting that the child inferred the model's original intentions.

2.2 Implicit False Belief Concept

A milestone in research on implicit ToM came from the violation-of-expectation (VOE) paradigm with looking time as the dependent variable to test if belief understanding develops in infancy. Poulin-Dubois et al. (1999) (see also Sodian et al., 2007) used the preferential-looking paradigm to test infants' concepts of knowledge versus ignorance. In one study, they reported that 18-month-old infants understand that an agent who wears a blindfold when the content of two boxes is revealed will not be cognizant of the location of an object when someone else asks for that information. This was revealed by the fact that infants looked longer when the agent pointed at the correct location. Poulin-Dubois (1999) also observed that infants looked longer at a protagonist who showed a surprised facial expression rather than a neutral expression when an object was no longer found where it was supposed to be. But Onishi and Baillargeon (2005) demonstrated that infants have an understanding of both true and false beliefs by using the VOE paradigm, designed initially to test infants' naïve understanding of physical principles such as support and gravity (Kellman & Spelke, 1983). The procedure required that infants first observe an agent hide an object inside one of two boxes and then reach for it repeatedly in a familiarization phase. An induction phase followed, during which the object moved from the original location to another location (the other box). The agent either witnessed the change (true belief condition) or disappeared behind a screen (false belief condition) during that critical event. During the test phase, the agent searched for the object either in the original location (congruent condition) or in the new location (incongruent condition; see Figure 3). Infants looked longer at a scene when the agent's behavior was incongruent with their true or false belief about a toy's location.

According to Onishi and Baillargeon, these results suggested that infants expected the agent to behave according to where the agent believed the toy to be hidden and not where the toy was actually hidden, indicating belief understanding. Following this landmark study, other tasks based on spontaneous responses (as opposed to elicited responses) have been designed to test false belief in

(a) Familiarization: Agent puts toy in dark box

(b) Change: Agent doesn't see toy move to lighter box

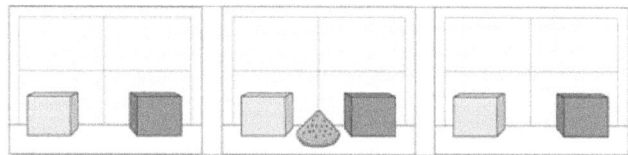

(c) Test events: Infant sees agent search, in either:

       Light box   Dark box

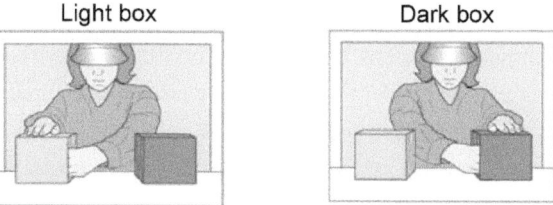

Figure 3 Depiction of the violation-of-expectation paradigm developed by Onishi and Baillargeon (2005). Figure reproduced from Wellman (2014) with permission.

preverbal infants. For example, Southgate and colleagues (2007) showed that 25-month-olds correctly performed anticipatory-looking behavior in a nonverbal false belief test, a procedure similar to that developed by Clements and Perner (1994) except that no interview was taking place. Another type of implicit measure of Theory of Mind is the interactive paradigm in which infants must assist an agent to find an object based on their understanding of the agent's knowledge, or lack thereof. For example, when an agent falsely believes that a desired object is in location x, 18-month-old infants spontaneously point to inform the agent that the object has been moved to another location or has been replaced with an aversive object (anticipatory-pointing tasks; Knudsen & Liszkowski, 2011). At the same age, infants will help an agent retrieve an object that is no longer where the agent thinks it is (Buttelmann et al., 2009). Toddlers also express more tension in their facial expressions when an agent who is approaching a container is mistaken, as opposed to ignorant, about its contents (affective-response tasks; Moll et al., 2016). In elicited-intervention tasks, children watch a scene in which an agent forms a false belief and then are asked to perform some action for the agent. Correct performance requires children to take into account the agent's false belief (for a review, see Scott & Baillargeon, 2017).

The road to uncovering infants' cognitive abilities has been paved by waves of methodological advances. The study of infants' Theory of Mind is no exception. However, measurement of early ToM has been surrounded with controversy. For example, infancy researchers have often used artificial stimuli (e.g., geometric figures) to study infants' understanding of mental states because of the experimental control that comes with them. However, simplified, artificial stimuli have led to questions about the validity of the empirical findings. The issue is whether many tasks have sufficient construct validity, more specifically measurement (or internal) validity, which refers to whether observed results are generated by infants' understanding of the construct that the researchers intended to study (Kominsky et al., 2022). Moreover, low measurement reliability, defined as the precision or the consistency of a specific instrument when a measurement is repeated, has plagued research on ToM in infancy when individual differences are investigated (see Byers-Heinlein et al., 2021, for solutions for more reliable infant research).

2.3 Is Early Theory of Mind Predictive of Later ToM?

Complementing studies testing infants' ToM, a body of work exists on the conceptual link between implicit (automatic, fast, and nonverbal) and explicit (slow, effortful, and verbal) understanding of mental states (see Sodian et al., 2020, for a review). Such an approach helps to identify the depth of ToM precursors in infancy, as one would expect strong predictive validity of early ToM if there is a full-fledged, mature ToM in infancy that is only detectable with implicit tasks, as posited by the mentalist or rich perspective on ToM in infancy. The first attempt to test this prediction focused on simple mental states such as goals/intentions in infancy and later ToM. Wellman and colleagues (2004) conducted a longitudinal study with children who had participated in a study on intentional action at 14 months. The infants had been administered a goal attribution task based on the paradigm designed by Woodward: After being habituated to an actor showing interest in one of two objects, test trials included a consistent event (actor grabbed the same toy) and an inconsistent event (actor grabbed another toy). At the age of 4 years, the children were administered the Wellman and Liu ToM scale. Unexpectedly, only a decrease in attention (i.e., how fast infants habituated), and not performance on the test trials, was positively related to performance on the ToM scale. The authors concluded that these findings provide some evidence for the predictive validity of sociocognitive abilities from infancy to childhood. In a follow-up study, Aschersleben and colleagues (2008) investigated whether infants' performance on a goal-directed action task, adapted again from the paradigm used by Woodward (1998), was correlated with their performance on the Wellman and Liu (2004) ToM scale years later. In the goal-directed action task, 6-month-old infants were habituated to an actor's hand pushing an object to a designated circle. Following this, infants viewed two types of test trials: a "path change" trial and an "object change" trial. Once again, infants' decrement of attention in the goal-directed action task was correlated with their scores at the age of 4 years on the combined false belief tasks. Yamaguchi and colleagues (2009) also investigated the link between 12-month-olds' understanding of goal-directed actions to their ToM understanding at 4 years of age, adding a nonsocial cognition task to the design, which allowed to demonstrate that the link was not general but domain-specific. In contrast to previous results, the link that they observed was between performance during the test events in the infants' task and later ToM and not between the decrement of attention during the familiarization task and later ToM.

Another body of work has focused on the link between early forms of intention understanding in infancy and more mature forms that emerge during the preschool period. Olineck and Poulin-Dubois (2007) found that intentional action understanding in 14- and 18-month-olds, which was measured with the reenactment of the intended acts task, predicted later intention understanding, as assessed with a target-hitting task at 4 years of age. Sodian and colleagues (2016) observed a significant pathway between intention understanding and later ToM, but the significant link was with infants' looking time preference on test events and not with habituation rate. Taken together, these studies suggest that goal and intention understanding in infancy are related to ToM constructs in childhood. However, the fact that the link was often restricted to decrement of attention in infancy casts doubt on the conclusions that early Theory of Mind, as opposed to domain-general speed of information processing, predicts later Theory of Mind. Furthermore, a study conducted with measures of joint attention reported that intentional action understanding did not emerge as a significant predictor of later ToM. The unique longitudinal pathway that emerged as significant was the one for initiating joint attention and a global score of ToM generated from a parental report (Brandone & Stout, 2023). These findings provide strong evidence for a robust stability between basic sociocognitive skills, such as joint attention, and later ToM (Brink et al., 2015; Nelson et al., 2008; Sodian & Kristen-Antonow, 2015). Relatedly, Ruffman and colleagues (2023) reported that exposure to repetitions of others' behaviors (e.g., searches for an object, repeated behaviors) during infants' first year correlated with children's acquisition of mental state words, even after controlling for their general vocabulary and a range of variables indexing social interaction. The authors interpreted these findings as providing support for a minimalist account of ToM in infancy. According to that view, infants initially understand others' behaviors but not their mental states (Perner, 2010; Perner & Ruffman, 2005).

A growing body of literature examines longitudinal associations between false belief understanding in infancy and childhood. In the first longitudinal study to test stability of false belief, Thoermer and colleagues (2011) tested a sample of German children on both an implicit and two explicit false belief tasks (content and location) at multiple time points. False belief understanding at 18 months of age, as measured with the anticipatory looking paradigm, predicted explicit location false belief (i.e., predicting where the actor will search for an object that moved when the actor was absent) as well as the sum score of both false belief tasks. They concluded that false belief, particularly as measured by a location false belief task, is stable over time. With data from the same sample, Sodian and colleagues (2016) also found that infants' goal understanding at 7 months and implicit false belief understanding at 18 months of age predicted 5-year-olds' ability to understand that an accidental transgressor could hold positive intentions. Thus, there seems to be longitudinal link between early understanding of mental states and the understanding of intentional agency involved in later moral judgment, providing additional support for a mentalistic view. With a group of children also drawn from the same sample, the same research group compared performance on an anticipatory-looking task measuring implicit false belief at 18 months, to explicit false belief understanding when children were 50, 60, and 70 months of age with content and location false belief tasks. Potential confounding variables (executive functions and verbal abilities) were also measured. Implicit false belief understanding was still significantly related to explicit false belief understanding even after controlling for verbal ability and executive functions. The score on the implicit false belief task explained 50% of variance (with executive functions) of false belief understanding at 4 and 5 years of age (Kloo et al., 2020). The authors of this longitudinal project concluded that there is an intrinsic relation between various measures of false belief understanding between 18 and 70 months. Sodian and colleagues (2024) examined the longitudinal stability of explicit false belief understanding from toddlerhood (33 months) to 4 years of age. Performance in a low-demand false belief task at 33 months of age (75% success rate) was significantly correlated with performance in a content false belief task at 52 months independent of language ability and executive function. Given that the majority of longitudinal studies on false belief had reported poor performance on the infants' task, this positive evidence of stability seems less plagued by problem of validity of implicit false belief tasks.

In their review of longitudinal studies of ToM development, Sodian and colleagues (2020) concluded that the current findings are consistent with the mentalistic, rich account of ToM. It is worth pointing out that the authors use the term "conceptual continuity" on ToM in the sense of consistency over time in performance on the measured constructs, not in the traditional definition of no change in group scores over time (Bornstein et al., 2017). They also believe that their data are compatible with the view that a preconceptual implicit mindreading system precedes an explicit ToM, endorsing a conceptual enrichment position. Regardless of the nature of conceptual continuity, they pointed out that their findings provide critical evidence against a strictly nonmentalistic account of infant psychological reasoning. Additionally, they concluded that "longitudinal data are needed to resolve controversies on foundational issues of the development of mindreading, and they can help us understand interrelations among fundamental processes of social cognitive development" (Sodian et al., 2020, p. 175). Although the aforementioned studies suggest that early implicit false belief understanding can predict explicit false belief understanding later in development (Kloo et al., 2020; Sodian et al., 2016; Thoermer et al., 2011), a number of studies have failed to replicate these findings or have reported a concurrent dissociation between the differential looking score (DLS) measure of the anticipatory looking task and explicit false belief (Grosse Wiesmann et al., 2018; Poulin-Dubois et al., 2020). Poulin-Dubois and colleagues (2020) tested the stability of ToM from infancy to childhood in two experiments. In the first experiment, they found no statistically significant correlations between performance on VOE tasks (i.e., false belief and goal-directed action tasks) at either 14 or 18 months of age and performance on implicit and explicit tasks (i.e., anticipatory looking and ToM Scale) at 4 or 5 years of age. In the second experiment, a false belief task and a knowledge attribution task were administered at 18 months. Then, the same children were tested with the ToM Scale at 5 years of age. Again, no associations between early and late ToM were found. In another study, Poulin-Dubois and colleagues (2023) combined the data reported in their 2020 paper with those of a follow-up experiment that tested the same constructs and replicated these null results. These results challenge the conclusion that explicit false belief reasoning develops from a precocious false belief concept that emerges early in infancy.

In summary, as discussed by Poulin-Dubois and Goldman (2023), existing longitudinal work is limited by modest sample sizes, invalid infant measures, and ToM assessments with restricted variability and generalizability. Future studies with such designs will most likely need to await valid, reliable measures of infants' false belief understanding that are currently being examined with multilaboratory projects such as those generated by the ManyBabies2 project that focus on the anticipatory looking paradigm (Schuwerk et al., 2025).

2.4 Infants' Theory of Mind: The Replication Crisis

The field of psychology, including developmental science, faces a replication crisis. Spearheaded by an informal compilation of published and unpublished non-replications (Kulke & Rakoczy, 2018), a special issue of the journal *Cognitive Development* was devoted to ToM research. It included several studies that reported failed attempts to replicate three tasks which were designed to measure implicit false belief and other ToM constructs in infancy (Sabbagh & Paulus, 2018). Some papers did not replicate the interactive, helping task, others did not replicate the well-known VOE task, and others failed to replicate the anticipatory-looking paradigm. Even the famous "broccoli" task assessing the understanding of subjective desires was among the failed replications (Ruffman et al., 2018).

In their invited commentary, the authors of the original experiments (Baillargeon, Buttelmann and Southgate) identified a number of procedural differences between the original studies and the replications that could explain the failures to replicate their original findings (Baillargeon et al., 2018). Similar arguments were addressed in the Open Collaboration project at the origins of the replication crisis in psychology (Gilbert et al., 2016). In their reply to this commentary, the authors of the papers included in the special issue acknowledged the methodological argument but also pointed out that the original findings might be false positives and that there is no justification to give them priority over later replication failures (Poulin-Dubois et al., 2018). They also pointed out that failed replications are informative as demonstrations of the fragility of some of the original findings. Soon after the publication of the special issue, 56 false belief conditions using the VOE, anticipatory looking, and interactive paradigms were included in a meta-analysis that included 1469 infants. Among the main findings, this meta-analysis revealed that, although infants performed these tasks above chance level, particularly VOE, there was much variability in the results (Barone et al., 2019). Results showed that the VOE paradigm had a significant mean effect size, $\beta = 1.28$, 95% CI [0.86; 1.69], which indicates that correct performance on the task was about 3.58 times more likely than incorrect performance. A significant mean effect size, $\beta = 0.31$, 95% CI [0.01; 0.61], was reported for the interactive paradigm, suggesting that correct performance on the task was about 1.36 times more likely than incorrect performance. By contrast, the meta-analysis for the anticipatory looking paradigm provided no significant mean effect size, $\beta = 0.16$, 95% CL [−0.24; 0.57]. The authors of this meta-analysis also reported a possible publication bias in this body of work and less positive findings in studies that have tested larger samples and included better control conditions. In fact, large effect sizes were found in early studies on implicit false belief attribution, but this outcome could not be replicated in more recent experiments. Relatedly, those large effect sizes were found with small samples, whereas later studies used bigger samples.

As part of the massive effort to replicate and expand studies providing the foundation for a rich ToM in infancy, conceptual replications have been conducted with the original VOE paradigm. The findings from these studies have forced a revision of the rich mentalistic account. For example, Burnside and colleagues (2020) conducted a study that was a conceptual replication of the VOE procedure, with a human agent replaced by an inanimate agent, a toy mechanical crane (see Figure 4). Infants watched the toy crane repeatedly move toward a box containing an object. In the absence of the crane, the object changed location. When the crane returned, 16-month-old infants looked longer when it turned toward the object's new location, consistent with the attribution of a false belief to the crane. These results suggest that infants spontaneously attribute false beliefs to inanimate agents, unlike adults who correctly expected the crane to "search"

Green-box condition (incongruent)

Yellow-box condition (congruent)

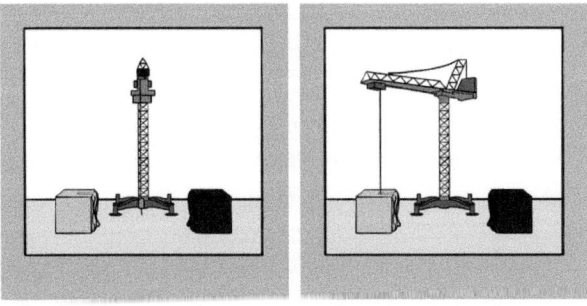

Figure 4 Depiction of the test events in the VOE task with a mechanical toy crane as the agent (figure reproduced from Burnside et al., 2020, with permission).

Theory of Mind in Childhood

for the object in the old location. Thus, infants overattribute mental states (if this is what they do in the VOE paradigm) to *any* agents.

Similarly, a conceptual replication of the classic false belief VOE task based on a switch agent paradigm revealed that 16-month-old infants attributed true and false beliefs to a naïve agent, an agent who had not been present during the familiarization phase and thus not cognizant of the original location of the object (Burnside et al., 2020). Therefore, they did not perceive beliefs as person-specific. Again, these findings indicate that the mechanisms that underlie infants' implicit attribution of beliefs might differ from those assumed for explicit reasoning about beliefs. They challenge the view that developmental changes in false belief understanding may be described as strengthening and enriching initial adult-like representations.

2.5 Theory of Mind in Infancy: New Directions

What can be concluded from the multiple non-replications of all implicit ToM tasks? Should some of the original paradigms, such as VOE, be abandoned to test false belief, as Paulus (2022) suggested? As mentioned earlier, although failed replications have been reported in many other areas of cognitive development, the large number of failed attempts in the case of early false belief understanding suggests that it might be very fragile or based on simple low-level processing. One possibility is that the original experiments, as well as failed replications, have only examined belief in nonevaluative contexts, in which an agent has beliefs about the location of an inanimate object or the content of a box (Woo et al., 2024). Thus, it is possible that neutral contexts do not motivate infants to care about agents' beliefs, leading to mixed results. In contrast, the authors suggest that socially evaluative contexts may facilitate belief representations by raising infants' motivation to care about agents' mental states. As an illustration, participants of all ages are able to form nonverbal belief representations when one agent chases another agent. This social goal may trigger social evaluation rather than a simple search for an object. For example, based on the design developed with adults by Heider and Simmel (1944), Surian and Franchin (2020) showed toddlers and adults videos of a triangle that chased a disk. The disk moved from one box to another in the presence or absence of the triangle. When the triangle returned, 20-month-old infants and adults, but not 15-month-olds, looked first to the location where the triangle last "saw" the disk. These findings contrast with failures to replicate findings of belief representations in infants and toddlers when an agent instead searches for an object. Woo and colleagues (2024) reported findings that appear to challenge the hypothesis that a precocious implicit understanding of others' beliefs about objects' locations and identities develops in infancy as well as the proposal that infants are altercentric, that is, have a sensitivity to the targets and contents of others' attention (Kampis & Southgate, 2020; Southgate, 2020). The basic design consisted of testing toddlers' understanding of the goals of an actor whose visual perspective of two pictures differed from their own during a familiarization phase and who selectively reached for or pointed to one member of the pair of pictures based on its orientation (upright versus inverted) or visibility (in front of versus behind an occluder). Looking time was used to measure toddlers' expectations about the agent's actions. Would the children encode the actor's goal according to the actor's perspective, with their own perspective throughout the event, or with neither perspective? When the toddlers and an actor viewed the same pictures of human faces or animal heads from different directions, toddlers interpreted the actor's actions on the pictures in accord with their own, rather than the actor's, experiences of the pictures. These findings support the proposal that there is a low-level system form of mental state reasoning (also called signature limit) that applies not only to toddlers but also to adults and young children in certain contexts (Butterfill & Apperly, 2013; Carey, 2009; Spelke, 2022).

3 Correlates of Theory of Mind

Many researchers assume that the development of false belief understanding during the preschool period is not an artifact of the task demands but rather a reflection of a genuine conceptual change that occurs during the preschool years (Wellman et al., 2001). If this is the case, then the question is how is such a progression explained? One hypothesis is that ToM achievements, from desires to second-order beliefs, reflect the gradual maturation of a ToM module, that is, an innate neural structure that has been honed and selected through evolution. Another hypothesis is that ToM development is the result of social experiences that vary across children. Decades of research have revealed that there is variability in the particular age at which, for example, individual children achieve success on false belief tasks, at 3 years of age for some children and not until 5 or 6 years for others. The fact that there is such individual variation in development has led researchers to explore possible correlates of false belief understanding in cognitive and social variables in both typically developing and clinical populations (Repacholi & Slaughter, 2003). Thus, a substantial body of research has accumulated about the determinants of ToM development, ranging from social to cognitive variables (Jenkins & Astington, 1996). The following sections attempt to cover the key findings in this vast domain of research, including the impact of language, family factors,

SES, language, executive functions, and bilingualism. It is important to point out that most correlates of ToM are moderate in strength and are often based on small sample sizes. Meta-analyses on this topic have highlighted the limited number of studies using cross-lagged designs and interventions to test causal links between ToM and various correlates (Devine & Hughes, 2014, 2018).

3.1 Language Skills

A large research literature demonstrates relations between language and ToM development; that is, children with more advanced language skills are also more advanced in ToM for both first-order and second-order false belief (Milligan et al., 2007). But what specific aspect of language development plays a role in ToM development? It appears that a variety of language measures has been identified as predictive of ToM: syntax, semantics, and pragmatics. Regarding syntax, de Villiers and de Villiers (2000, 2009) proposed that the mastery of embedded complement clauses (e.g., John thinks that . . .) supports the development of the concept of belief. Both longitudinal and training studies suggest a causal relation between linguistic abilities and mentalizing abilities, with the former influencing the latter. In neurotypical preschoolers, the mastery of complements, such as "John thinks that the chocolate is in the drawer", is predictive of ToM (Astington & Jenkins, 1999; de Villiers & Pyers, 2002; Hale & Tager-Flusberg, 2003; Lohmann & Tomasello, 2003). Sentential complements (sentences introduced by the complementizer "that") arguably serve as ideal tools for the representation of metarepresentations because they show someone else's point of view (de Villiers, 2007). In their meta-analysis, Milligan et al. (2007) reported that complementation skills ranked above other linguistic abilities, such as global syntax or receptive vocabulary, in predicting ToM performance. A training study reported that sentential complements were beneficial for addressing ToM difficulties in children with ASD, especially those with milder symptoms (Durrleman et al., 2022). However, a longitudinal study with 3-year-olds and three false belief tasks, a working memory task, and four language tasks (each designed to tap a different aspect of syntax or semantics), were administered twice at 6-month intervals (Slade & Ruffman, 2005). A bidirectional relation between language and ToM was observed, but no one measure of syntax or semantics was more likely than any other to predict later false belief. Regarding the reverse causal link, the authors reported that false belief was no more related to one aspect of later language (syntax vs. semantics) than another. These findings are consistent with the idea that both syntax and semantics contribute to understanding false beliefs. Additional studies have confirmed that language predicts later ToM, but they have cast doubt on the unique importance of syntax. Farrar and Maag (2002) obtained parent-report measures of vocabulary size and expressive grammatical complexity, as well as MLU, when children were 27 months old, then measured ToM at age 4 years, using appearance-reality, unexpected contents, and change of location tasks. Vocabulary and MLU predicted ToM performance, but grammatical complexity was not a predictor when they controlled for vocabulary. Ruffman and colleagues (2003) compared measures of syntax and semantics at age 3 as predictors of ToM performance at ages 3, 4, and 5 years. Semantic ability accounted for unique variance in understanding of belief, but syntactic ability did not account for additional variance. Finally, Watson et al. (2001) found that verbal competence at 24 months (e.g., vocabulary, sentence complexity, grammar) predicted false belief understanding (content task) at 48 months. It seems clear that language and ToM performance are related and that language is a better predictor of ToM than the reverse.

So, what can be concluded about this very strong claim about the developmental role of one syntactic structure? It has been challenged in a number of ways. First, it has been argued that diverse beliefs and false belief tasks both require the same sort of syntactic structures. Yet, there is a developmental lag between the two ToM constructs, with diverse beliefs acquired before false beliefs (Wellman et al., 2001). The second argument against this strong claim comes from cross-linguistic studies, particularly ToM development in children speaking non-English languages with no or little complementation, such as Cantonese or Mandarin. In such languages, the same grammatical construction is used to discuss desire and belief. Yet, the order of acquisition of these mental states is the same as English-speaking children (Liu et al., 2008; Tardif & Wellman, 2000; Wellman et al., 2006).

3.2 Family Factors

A wide range of family factors impact ToM development, with a focus on false belief understanding. Those factors include number of siblings, parents' use of mental state language, mind-mindedness, parenting style, and attachment. In a longitudinal study of toddlers and their mothers, Dunn and colleagues (1991) observed that variation in the frequency of talk about feelings at the age of 33 months predicted false belief understanding 7 months later. This study launched a wave of research on potential social influences on children's false belief understanding that is summarized in a book by Miller (2016) as well as in a meta-analysis covering 25 years of research on both distal (SES and the number of siblings) and proximal (mental state language and mind-mindedness) family correlates of false belief reasoning (Devine & Hughes, 2018). Overall, these studies have shown the false belief construct exhibited modest associations with each family variable, and these associations held even when individual differences in children's verbal ability were considered. Analyses including moderators revealed that key child-related factors (e.g., age, gender) as well as methodological factors amplified or attenuated relations between each family variable and false belief.

3.2.1 Siblings

Regarding the impact of siblings, researchers have explored its impact on ToM by examining the effect of having siblings or not, their age, and a larger kin group. The first study to provide evidence that sibling relationships might play a key role in ToM focused on FB (Dunn et al., 1991). In a longitudinal design, toddlers aged 33 months who frequently engaged in cooperative play with an older sibling performed better on a false belief task 7 months later. Perner and colleagues (1994) then reported that having one or more siblings, older or younger, compared with having none, provided an advantage in false belief performance. Jenkins and Astington (1996) replicated this finding and found that family size, regardless of birth order, age, and verbal skills, significantly predicted false belief understanding in young children. The last two studies showed a linear effect of siblings: That is, false belief performance improved as much between no siblings and one sibling as it did between one sibling and two siblings. In order to test the generalizability of this effect, Ruffman and colleagues (1998) examined the impact of older versus younger siblings in a large sample of English and Japanese children. They found no advantage associated with younger siblings but significantly higher scores among children with older siblings. Furthermore, the youngest group of children (aged 3 years) with older siblings showed no such advantage, which suggested a lower age limit for older siblings to influence ToM development.

The nature of the sibling effect was also investigated by Peterson (2000) with a design that considered both the age of the siblings and the birth order. Birth order was found to be irrelevant, provided that the younger siblings were aged at least 12 months and there was no benefit associated with older siblings above the age of 13 years. This led Peterson to conclude that what is important is that children have others with whom to interact. Peterson also created a sibling variety score with points awarded for having at least one younger sibling over 12 months of age, 1 point for having at least one older sibling younger than 13 years and for having a twin, as well as 0.5 points for having at least one sibling aged 13 years or older. Children's sibling variety scores predicted a significant additional amount of the variance in false belief understanding beyond control variables such as age, language skills, and number of siblings. In summary, rather than absolute age or relative birth order, the variety of siblings provides a benefit for ToM within a particular age range. Longitudinal links observed between child–sibling numbers and higher scores on standard ToM tests are consistent with a direction of influence from child siblings to advanced mental state understanding (McAlister & Peterson, 2007).

Not all studies have found a relation between having siblings (older or younger) and competence at ToM tasks (Cole & Mitchell, 2000; Cutting & Dunn, 1999; Peterson & Slaughter, 2003). As suggested by Cutting and Dunn (1999), the quality of sibling interaction might be more important than the number of siblings. Pretend play between siblings, for example, has been associated with the use of internal state language (Howe et al., 1998; Howe et al., 2002; Youngblade & Dunn, 1995), and this increased talk about mental states may be an important mechanism in the development of ToM. Furthermore, pretend play with older siblings may facilitate the ability to distinguish reality from representations of reality, which has positive effects on false belief performance (Ruffman et al., 1998).

3.2.2 Parental Mind-Mindedness

Mind-mindedness is another social factor that is related to individual differences in ToM development. Mind-mindedness refers to a tendency to treat young children as psychological agents with their own minds (e.g., McMahon & Bernier, 2017; Meins et al., 2002, 2003; Sharp & Fonagy, 2008). The measure of mind-mindedness varies as a function of the child's age. In infancy, it is measured by recording mental state comments during parent–child interactions. At older ages, parents' descriptions of their child are used to identify the number of references to the child's mental life (Meins et al., 1998, 2013). A large number of studies and comprehensive reviews have provided evidence that fathers' and mothers' appropriate mind-minded (MM) comments to their children, that is, comments that accurately reference the child's mental states (desires, emotions, beliefs), facilitate the development of ToM (e.g., de Rosnay et al., 2004; Devine & Hughes, 2013; McMahon & Bernier, 2017; Meins et al., 2013; Pavarini et al., 2013; Tompkins et al., 2018). A meta-analysis conducted by Aldrich and colleagues (2021) examined the stability of the relation between parental mind-mindedness and children's executive functions and social cognition by reviewing a sample of 42 studies. Parental mind-mindedness was most strongly correlated with children's executive functions, language abilities, and social cognition, particularly during toddlerhood. Relations were shown both concurrently during the preschool period and prospectively, comparing measures taken in infancy and later ToM. Notably, the link has been established for a wide range of ToM outcomes and by considering potential confounding variables, such as the child's language. This body of work concludes that parents who rank relatively high in mind-mindedness have children who rank relatively high in ToM. However, a few studies have failed to observe this link, probably because they focused on concurrent relations in infancy (Dunphy-Lelii et al., 2014; Licata et al., 2014) or diverged in their procedure and scoring system from previous studies (Ereky-Stevens, 2008).

3.2.3 Mental State Talk

Another proximal factor that could impact ToM is mental state language that children are exposed to from parents and others. Mental state language is measured by recording the number of times that parents use words referring to cognition (e.g., think), desires (e.g., want), and emotions (e.g., happy) when interacting with their children. Mental state language has been suggested as a candidate to account for the fact that mind-mindedness seems to nurture the development of ToM, but it remains to be seen how such talk produces its effect and whether mind-mindedness can be reduced to mental state language. A substantial literature shows clear concurrent and predictive relations between the quantity and quality of mental state talk and ToM, regardless of mind-mindedness (Dunn et al., 1991; Ensor & Hughes, 2008; Ruffman et al., 2002). Furthermore, training studies strongly suggest that the causal relation is from mental state talk to children's understanding of mental states. These studies have shown that children who took part in mental state conversations about stories showed greater improvements in ToM than children who listened to the same stories but did not take part in mental state conversations (Bianco et al., 2016; Lecce et al., 2014; Ornaghi et al., 2011, 2014). But is mental state talk the same construct as mind-mindedness? It appears that it is not. In a study that attempted to tease apart these variables, preschoolers and their parents were studied across a 13-month period. The main findings indicated little overlap in parental mind-mindedness, mental state talk, and Theory of Mind capacity. Importantly, only mental state talk predicted later false belief reasoning (Devine & Hughes, 2019). The main reason is that mental state talk is an expression of mind-mindedness, but it is only one way in which mind-mindedness can be expressed. For example, it is measured as the appropriate scaffolding during problem-solving, including a number of behaviors by which parents can respond appropriately to their child's mental state. Mind-mindedness is related to a number of aspects of parenting that impact child development, including ToM. For example, parents who score high in mind-mindedness tend to display high levels of sensitivity (Demers et al., 2010; Licata et al., 2014; Meins et al., 2012).

3.2.4 Parenting Style

Parenting style is how parents interact, discipline, communicate, and respond to the behavior of a child. A substantial literature relates parenting style and ToM (Cahill et al., 2007; Farrant et al., 2012; Holmes-Lonergan, 2003; Hughes et al., 1999; Lewis et al., 2006; Olson et al., 2011; Pears & Moses, 2003; Ruffman et al., 1999; Shahaeian et al., 2014; Vinden, 2001). As is the case for correlational studies, it cannot be established if a causal relation exists between parental style and children's ToM. Although it is assumed that parental style impacts a child's ToM, the reverse could be true; that is, children with an advanced ToM might elicit particular behaviors in their parents. As is always the case with correlational designs, a third factor might explain the relation, such as shared genes, with intelligent parents passing genes linked to higher IQ to their children who would then perform well on a range of cognitive tests, including ToM. Nonetheless, the rationale guiding the research on parenting styles has been that the authoritative style will be beneficial, and the authoritarian style will be detrimental for ToM development. This pattern has been reported in many aspects of child development, as explained by the fact that authoritative parents emphasize reasoning and discussion, unlike authoritarian parents who value strict punishment and poor communication. Overall, this research has confirmed the hypothesis that the authoritative parenting style benefits ToM, although the evidence is not overwhelming. Among the first studies to report a positive link between authoritative parenting style and ToM is Ruffman and colleagues (1999). The concept of false belief at the ages of 3 and 4 years was predicted by maternal disciplinary responses that stressed the effect of children's actions on other people's emotions and the tendency to reprimand, which were related negatively to the construct. Subsequent studies have confirmed these findings (Cahill et al., 2007; Farrant et al., 2012; Olson et al., 2011). Vinden (2001) developed the Parenting Attitudes Inventory, a self-report instrument, to assess dimensions such as encouragement of autonomy, behavioral control, and freedom in learning, and tested samples of Korean American and European American children. As expected, a negative relation emerged between mothers' endorsement of behavioral control and ToM understanding in their children, but only for European American children. A number of subsequent studies have confirmed these results, some replicating the fact that patterns reported in Western samples do not necessarily generalize to Asian cultures (Hughes & Ensor, 2006; Hughes et al., 1999; O'Reilly & Peterson, 2014; Olson et al., 2011; Pears & Moses, 2003; Shahaeian et al., 2011). Research on this topic has generated either null or conflicting results. Some have reported sex differences, such as a positive effect of discipline on a ToM battery only for boys (Hughes et al., 1999) or for both sexes when understanding of emotions is the outcome (Pears & Moses, 2003).

In summary, parenting style (warmth, reasoning, and discussion) appears to boost ToM development and harsh control hinders it. However, a number of studies report null or conflicting results and effect sizes tend to be modest.

3.2.5 Attachment

A final family factor that has been linked to ToM is attachment, a construct central to the parenting literature. A clear relation obtains between secure attachment and better social and cognitive development (Fearon et al., 2010; Groh et al., 2017; Sroufe, 2005; van Ijzendoorn et al., 1995). The quality of the early bond between parent and child predicts social competence (Ainsworth & Bowlby, 1991; Bretherton, 1985) and provides the building block for developmental competencies that interact within and across domains (Masten & Cicchetti, 2010). Bretherton (1985, 1990) linked attachment theory to the development of a Theory of Mind. She argued that, in contrast to insecurely attached children, securely attached children are able to devote more attention to experiences that help acquire knowledge about the mind. Speculations about a specific link with ToM can be found at the beginning of the research on ToM (Fonagy et al., 1991; Main, 1991). In the first longitudinal study designed to test the relation between quality of attachment and mindreading performance, Fonagy and his colleagues (Fonagy et al., 1991; Steele et al., 1996) reported that security of attachment at the age of 12 months predicted Theory of Mind at the age of 5 years, as measured with false belief and cognitive-emotion tasks. Secure attachment in infancy with mother predicted success in the cognitive-emotion task. Since then, studies have addressed the role of attachment in ToM. Although many discuss the link between attachment and ToM (Dykas & Cassidy, 2011; Pavarini et al., 2013; see also book chapters: Hughes, 2011; Meins, 2012), most only provide a qualitative synthesis. Only through meta-analyses is it possible to detect general trends across studies and estimate mean effect sizes. In such a meta-analytic review of the attachment-ToM association, Szpak and Bialeka-Pikul (2020) concluded, based on 12 studies, that attachment security related to better ToM skills. However, the effect size of this association was moderate. The authors of this meta-analysis concluded that future studies are required to investigate such a link, given that attachment impacts other correlates of ToM. Finally, the specific developmental mechanisms underlying these links require future examination.

3.3 Socioeconomic Status

A global/distal social influence on ToM is socioeconomic status (SES). SES is a multifaceted construct that is often indexed by parental or family income, occupation, or educational attainment, or some combination of those measures

(Conger & Donnellan, 2007). The association between family SES and children's cognitive development has received much attention in the child development literature (Duncan & Magnuson, 2012; Farah, 2017; Hackman & Farah, 2009; Moriguchi & Shinorama, 2019). The potential influence of SES on ToM was largely overlooked because there was limited variability in the small and middle-class samples of children usually studied. Extant results are mixed. Although a number of studies suggest that higher levels of parental education and occupational prestige are linked with children's more rapid ToM mastery (Cole & Mitchell, 1998; Ebert et al., 2017; Ruffman et al., 2002; Ruffman et al., 2006), other studies report no such link (Adrián et al., 2005, 2007; Dunn et al., 1991; Murray et al., 1999; Pears & Moses, 2003; Ruffman et al., 1999; Tompkins, 2015). There are many reasons for such discrepancies, including characteristics of the samples as well as how the SES variable was operationalized. For example, Hughes and colleagues (1998) observed an association between paternal occupational status as well as maternal education and children's ToM. However, this association only held for typically developing children, but not for children at risk for behavior disorders. In addition, various SES indicators (like household income) might be confounded with (poor) parental mental and physical health, including greater parental stress and reduced social support. To illustrate that point, Guajardo and colleagues (2009) showed that household income and self-reported life stress, but not parental education, predicted children's ToM scores.

In their meta-analysis of the family factors related to ToM, Devine and Hughes (2019) concluded, based on data from thousands of families from 11 different countries, that there is a modest correlation between family SES and individual differences in false belief reasoning. Although modest, the association held even when individual differences in children's verbal ability were taken into account. Also, the correlation between family SES and children's FB was stronger for older children and the effect sizes reported in their analysis were overall weaker than those reported for the relations between FB and language (Milligan et al., 2007) or executive function (Devine & Hughes, 2014).

In summary, family factors have been linked to ToM, and particularly false belief understanding. Devine and Hughes (2018) compiled the data from 93 studies of 3- to 7-year-old children to extract the correlations between false belief and four family factors: parental socioeconomic status, number of siblings, parental mental state talk, and mind-mindedness. They reported modest, but statistically significant, associations between false belief and each family factor. Individual differences in verbal ability did not account for these associations. They also observed that child-related factors (e.g., age, gender) as well as methodological factors (e.g., proportion vs raw measures of mental talk) moderated the strength of relations between false belief and each family factor. Finally, longitudinal data confirmed that family factors play a causal role in the development of that construct, although this conclusion is based on a small number of studies with false belief measures at more than one time point.

3.4 Culture

Culture refers to a group's set shared values, practices, and beliefs. Culture is an overarching factor that is likely to impact most social forces reviewed so far. For example, cultural values and beliefs likely impact whether parents engage in mental talk and mind-mindedness. As Peterson and Slaughter (2017) pointed out, studying potential cross-cultural differences in children's ToM can have important theoretical implications: Universality of ToM development would provide support for biological maturation as the key developmental process, whereas variability across cultural groups would provide support for the role of social factors. The bulk of cross-cultural research on ToM development has focused on two key aspects of ToM development: One concerns the universality of ToM constructs (e.g., is there a culture where false belief does not develop?), and the other is the timing of ToM development (e.g., do children in different cultural groups acquire ToM at different times in development?). The first issue was examined by Avis and Harris (1991), who studied the timing of false belief understanding (location) in British versus West African preschoolers. Their results provided support for the claim that belief-desire reasoning develop similarly in both groups, in terms of both content and timing. Callaghan and colleagues (2005) also observed synchrony in the onset of mentalistic reasoning, with children mastering a standardized test of false belief at approximately 5 years of age in five distinct cultural groups (India, Peru, Samoa, Canada, and Thailand). Regarding the issue of timing, in their meta-analysis, Wellman and colleagues (2001) observed some variation in children from the Europe, North America, South America, East Asia, Australia, and Africa. Specifically, both Japanese and Peruvian children were slower to master false beliefs. In another meta-analysis, Liu and colleagues (2008) compared false belief performance in four locations (the United States, Canada, Hong Kong, and Beijing) that included several thousand children. Unexpectedly, as shown in Figure 5, Chinese children from Hong Kong were approximately 2 years slower than Canadian and American children despite sharing many aspects of their culture with the Chinese children. The authors offered two plausible hypotheses about how social factors might explain such differences in ToM timing. First, the Hong Kong children were more likely than the Beijing children to have siblings. As discussed earlier, having siblings predicts faster ToM mastery. A second

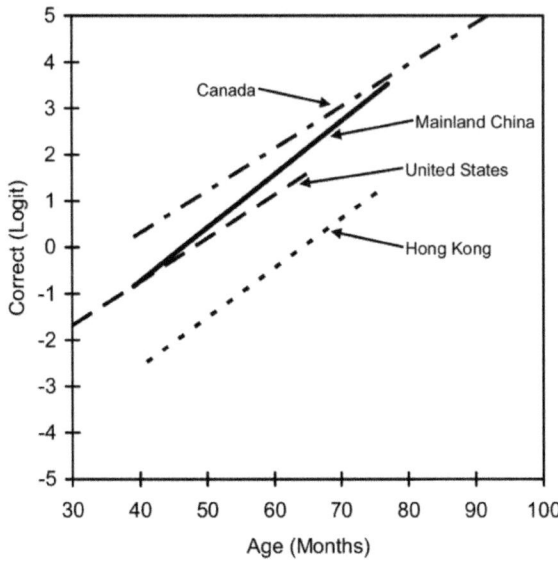

Figure 5 Developmental trajectory of false belief reasoning in five countries (figure reproduced from Liu et al., 2008, with permission).

possibility is that the Hong Kong children were more likely to be bilingual than the other samples, and there is some evidence that bilingualism is linked to ToM. In their review, Slaughter and Perez-Zapata (2014) concluded that the research indicates that in all cultures studied, individuals begin to attribute false beliefs to others in childhood but that there are cultural differences in the age at which children acquire this skill. It is not yet clear what accounts for these differences. Because most studies do not systematically measure variables such as bilingualism and family size, one or more of them, rather than culture, may account for some of the cross-cultural differences.

All the studies reviewed so far on culture and ToM focused on false belief reasoning, considered a marker of ToM. A comprehensive test of cross-cultural differences requires a similar investigation of the sequence of developmental milestones as documented by Wellman and Liu (2004) in their five-step scale of ToM acquisition. Does the same developmental sequence apply to children growing up in different socio-cultural contexts? Wellman and colleagues (2006) compared Chinese children with Australian and US American children. All children passed the ToM steps in the same sequence, but a cultural difference was observed in the order of acquisition of the tasks within the scale, with the Chinese children mastering the knowledge access and the diverse belief items in reversed order from Western children. Additional evidence of cross-cultural variation in the order of the

ToM scale concepts was observed when Iranian children were compared to Australian children (Shahaeian et al., 2011). Similarly to the pattern of results reported for Chinese children, Iranian children passed the diverse beliefs item before the knowledge access item despite an overall rate of ToM mastery that was identical across the two groups. A total of 10 studies have been published using the ToM scale to examine the order of emergence of ToM concepts in non-Western children (see Peterson & Slaughter, 2017, for a review). The general conclusion of this body of work is that there is cultural variation if only false belief scores are considered. However, there is substantial cross-cultural uniformity when the overall sequence of ToM is considered, except for the ordering of knowledge access and diverse belief (Yu and Wellman, 2024). Researchers have also reported slight delays in the ages at which children succeed at false belief tasks in collectivist Asian societies such as Japan (Wellman et al., 2001), Hong-Kong (Liu et al., 2008), and Pacific Island countries (e.g., Samoa; Mayer & Träuble, 2013). These findings have been attributed primarily to children's low levels of exposure to different beliefs because collectivist societies value mutual agreement, group harmony, and cohesion, which require believing in the same thing or acting in the same way.

In summary, this research shows that cultural norms and children's social experiences, which are guided by those norms, impact the age of acquisition and order of different mental state understanding. Both universal (e.g., the timing of false belief understanding) and socioculturally specific (e.g., variability in ToM sequences) findings are reported with respect to children's developmental timing and progression of ToM (Selcuk et al., 2023).

3.5 Cognitive Factors

3.5.1 Executive Functions

ToM abilities change dramatically during the preschool period, synchronized with similar changes in other aspects of cognition, such as executive functions. Executive functions (EFs) "make possible mentally playing with ideas; taking the time to think before acting; meeting novel, unanticipated challenges; resisting temptations; and staying focused" (Diamond, 2013, p. 1). Three-component processes have been identified as involved in EFs (Garon et al., 2008; Miyake et al., 2000): working memory (i.e., the ability to hold and manipulate information in mind), inhibition (i.e., the ability to suppress irrelevant responses), and shifting (i.e., the ability to change flexibly to new responses).

During the preschool years, individual differences in executive function abilities predict individual differences in ToM skills. Among typically developing 3- to 6-year-olds, individual differences in executive functions and false belief are related (e.g., Carlson & Moses, 2001; Frye et al., 1995; Hala et al., 2003; Hughes,

1998; Perner et al., 2002). For example, children with good perspective-taking skills tend to have good self-regulatory skills. Furthermore, there are deficits in both ToM and executive functions in atypical populations like children with ASD (Jones et al., 2017; Ozonoff & McEvoy, 2008; Pellicano, 2007). A meta-analysis of over 100 studies revealed a moderate, but significant, association between normative variation in executive functions and in false belief, with approximately 15% shared variance (Devine & Hughes, 2014). Moreover, these relations typically persist when variables such as age, verbal ability, and general cognitive ability are held constant (Carlson & Moses, 2001; Carlson et al., 2002; Carlson et al., 2004). Although a concurrent relation between ToM and EF has been reported, such convergence seems to improve with age, with the effect weaker in infancy and toddlerhood (e.g., Carlson and Moses, 2001; Carlson et al., 2004; Frye et al., 1995; Hughes, 1998; Hughes & Ensor, 2005, 2007; Perner & Lang, 1999; Poulin-Dubois & Yott, 2014). However, there is a consensus that these skills are related but distinct, as documented in a neuropsychological study by Sabbagh and colleagues (2009). Although EF and ToM were correlated in their study, activity in the dorsal medial prefrontal cortex and the right temporal–parietal juncture was associated with ToM even after controlling statistically for associations with EF. This provides evidence that the neural substrate of ToM reasoning is dissociable from EF reasoning (see also Sabbagh et al., 2006, for additional evidence in a cross-cultural study).

This body of work has led researchers to propose many possibilities for how ToM development might be explained by general cognitive development, such as executive functioning (Moses & Tahiroglu, 2010). One possibility is that a third cognitive variable links EF and ToM (e.g., Andrews et al., 2003; Frye et al., 1995; Frye et al., 1998). For example, reasoning by using hierarchically embedded rules is required to be successful in many ToM and EF tasks. According to this view, both types of tasks require the implementation of a higher-order rule to select the condition or the perspective that is relevant in a reasoning context (e.g., shifting rule in the Dimensional Change Card Sort task or perspective in false belief task). A second possibility is that ToM development is responsible for EF development (Perner & Lang, 1999; Perner et al., 2002). For example, it may be that understanding mental states is necessary to monitor or control those states. Perner and colleagues (2002) argued that metarepresentational capacities may be required for certain executive functions, such as inhibitory control. In other words, how can goals and desires be inhibited without understanding these mental states? A third possibility is a reverse pattern, with EF playing a minor role, such as allowing for the expression of preexisting ToM concepts (Carlson et al., 1998; Russell et al., 1991). For example, failure of the classic false belief task (Wimmer & Perner,

1983) might be a performance problem, not a competence problem, as a child might have already mastered the concept but does not yet possess the executive function skills to express that knowledge. (This is a key argument of proponents of the rich, mentalistic view of ToM.) In other words, in the false belief task, although the child knows where the object is located, the protagonist has a false belief concerning the final location of the object, given that the protagonist was absent when the object was moved. Thus, children might incorrectly answer this question because they may lack the inhibitory control skills required to avoid answering where the object currently is. In short, children would have a performance deficit as opposed to a competence deficit. A final possibility is that EF might be necessary for the emergence of ToM (Moses, 2001; Russell, 1996). For example, to shift perspectives, children must possess inhibitory control and working memory skills. According to this view, children might suffer from a conceptual deficit caused, at least in part, by insufficient executive capacity.

Does accumulated empirical evidence favor one of these accounts? There is strong support for the expression account, given the numerous studies suggesting a precocious ToM in infancy, but other findings provide strong support for the emergence account. Some support for the developmental primacy of EF first came from a study of children with autism (Pellicano, 2007) that revealed a dissociation between these skills, with ToM impaired but EF intact. Longitudinal studies have converged in showing that EF skills are necessary for later ToM development and not the reverse (Carlson et al., 2004; Flynn et al., 2004; Hughes, 1998; Hughes & Ensor, 2007; Schneider et al., 2005). Two studies included large and diversified samples. Marcovitch and colleagues (2015) conducted a longitudinal study that tested a large sample of socioeconomically and racially diverse children between 3 and 5 years of age and reported an asymmetrical pattern that persisted over two time points: EF at 3 years predicted ToM at 4 years, and EF at 4 years predicted ToM at 5 years. However, ToM did not predict EF between any two time points. So, as the nature of ToM changes with age, more complex EF skills must first develop. In addition, Kloo and colleagues (2020) measured ToM at 18 months with an implicit FB task (anticipatory looking), then explicit first-order and second-order false belief concepts at 50, 60, and 70 months, as well as executive functions assessed with eight different tasks that measured inhibitory skills. False belief understanding was related to executive functioning but not associated with implicit false belief understanding (see also Grosse Wiesmann et al., 2017; Low, 2010; Schuwerk et al., 2016; Zmyj et al., 2015). The most plausible explanation for their findings was the expression account of ToM development that proposes that to pass the explicit false belief task children must inhibit a prepotent tendency to answer the test question based on their own knowledge (the current location) in order to explicitly take the protagonist's perspective. In contrast to these findings, at least two studies have found a link between implicit FB and executive functioning in cross-sectional designs (Schneider et al., 2012; Yott & Poulin-Dubois, 2012). However, given that the object was not removed from the scene in those studies, it might have created higher inhibitory control demands (Grosse Wiesmann et al., 2017; Zmyj et al., 2015). Based on their meta-analytic review of 102 studies that examined the association between EF and ToM in children aged 3 to 6 years, Devine and Hughes (2014) concluded that there is a moderate association between these two constructs across cultures and distinct EF tasks but not across false belief tasks. Furthermore, the results of the few longitudinal ($N = 10$) and training ($N = 1$) studies included in the review made the authors conclude that early individual differences in EF predict later FB and not the reverse, supporting a hybrid emergence-expression theoretical account against the conceptual account.

Finally, training studies represent a uniquely informative way to examine EF–ToM relations, especially with respect to causal direction. If EF plays a causal role in this relation, then training on EF might be expected to enhance ToM. Conversely, if ToM is causal, then training on ToM might enhance EF. Only one study of this type has been carried out with typically developing children. Kloo and Perner (2003) trained 3- and 4-year-old children either on EF tasks (DCCS task) or ToM tasks (specifically unexpected transfer false belief). EF training led to better EF performance and to better ToM performance; ToM training led to enhanced EF performance, but surprisingly ToM training failed to enhance ToM performance. In another training study, preschool children who performed poorly on false belief tasks were enrolled in a training study designed to improve their performance on these tasks. The main objective was to determine whether children's growth in ToM was predicted by their performance on a battery of EF tasks. Individual differences in EF performance strongly and consistently predicted improvement in children's false belief performance both during the training period and during the posttest. These findings held after statistically controlling for several relevant covariates. The authors concluded that EF skills promote development in ToM by facilitating the ability to reflect on and learn from relevant experience (Benson et al., 2013). Longitudinal studies with older children have also reported an asymmetric developmental relation between EF and ToM, with working memory as the main instrumental EF component (Austin et al., 2014; Lecce et al., 2017). Finally, exploring whether similar relations between EF and ToM are present in diverse cultures can inform us about the nature of EF–ToM relations. If the relation is present in some cultures but not in others, then that would clearly rule out the hypothesis that EF is necessary for ToM or vice versa. To this date, only a small number of cross-cultural studies have been conducted, and all have found significant relations between EF and ToM across cultures (Sabbagh et al., 2006).

3.5.2 Bilingualism

The idea that bilingualism might benefit the development of ToM has a long history. It was first investigated by Goetz (2003), who tested 4-year-olds with standard ToM, such as appearance-reality, Level 2 perspective taking, and false belief tasks. The sample included English- and Mandarin-Chinese-speaking monolinguals and Mandarin-Chinese bilinguals with early dual language exposure and high proficiency. The bilinguals performed better than the monolingual groups, and three accounts were offered to explain such an advantage: greater inhibitory control, greater metalinguistic understanding, and greater sensitivity to sociolinguistic interactions with interlocutors. A meta-analysis of 16 studies reported a small-to-medium bilingual ToM advantage (Schroeder, 2018). In 24 empirical studies that investigated ToM development in bilingual children (Yu et al., 2021), the majority used false belief tasks or those tasks combined with other ToM tasks. Only 5 studies found no ToM advantage out of the 21 studies that included a control group of monolinguals, confirming the findings of the earlier meta-analysis (Schroeder, 2018).

How might bilingualism promote ToM development? Since proposed by Goetz, the three accounts have not been evaluated in light of existing research. Thus, it remains unknown whether any of these accounts or their combinations explain the ToM advantage associated with bilingualism. Regarding the executive functions account, working memory and inhibitory control fully mediate the significant relation between bilingualism and ToM (Bialystok & Senman, 2004; Nguyen & Astington, 2014). However, other studies have yielded null (or opposite) findings, failing to support an executive function account of the bilingual cognitive advantage (Buac & Kaushanskaya, 2020; Dahlgren et al., 2017; Fan et al., 2015). For example, Diaz and Farrar (2018a) observed that executive function abilities, specifically inhibitory control, predicted preschoolers' ToM but only in monolinguals, not bilinguals. This result was confirmed in a follow-up study with a longitudinal design with executive function at Time 1 associated with ToM at Time 2, but only in monolinguals (Diaz & Farrar, 2018b). In conclusion, empirical data provide inconsistent evidence for, and often clear evidence against, the executive functions account. Only a few studies have examined the relation between metalinguistic awareness and ToM in bilingual children (Diaz & Farrar, 2018b). Findings point to such a link, but more research is needed. Finally, the link between sociolinguistic awareness and ToM has also been rarely studied, but two studies suggest a positive relation (Cheung et al., 2010; Tare & Gelman, 2010).

In summary, none of the three accounts of the impact of bilingualism on Theory of Mind development claims that bilingualism enhances processes required for the development of ToM, but all support the conclusion that bilingualism simply provides more opportunities to develop the skills (i.e., metalinguistic awareness, sociolinguistic awareness, and executive functions) that advantage ToM learning.

3.6 Consequences of ToM Development

Alongside the literature on the determinants of Theory of Mind development, a solid body of work exists on the consequences of Theory of Mind for other aspects of child development, such as moral reasoning, social competence, and academic achievement. Regarding the impact of Theory of Mind on moral reasoning, the bulk of research has focused on lying, which is a reflection of children's cognitive ability to deceive rather than an intentional act of moral violation during the preschool years. Meta-analyses incorporating hundreds of studies with children aged 2–14 years have revealed that ToM is modestly but significantly linked to children's initial lies and their subsequent attempts to ensure their lies are convincing and undetectable by the lie-recipient (Babu et al., 2023; Lee & Imuta, 2021; Sai et al., 2021). Regarding social competence, in school-aged children teacher-rated social competence is associated with individual differences in both ToM and children's motivation to develop and maintain social relationships (Devine & Apperly, 2022). Data based largely on 3- to 6-year-old typically developing children point to associations between ToM and prosocial behavior (Imuta et al., 2016), peer popularity (Slaughter et al., 2015), and reciprocated friendship (Fink et al., 2015). Finally, in addition to supporting children's social interactions, individual differences in ToM benefit academic achievement, in particular reading comprehension and scientific reasoning (Lecce & Devine, 2021).

4 Theoretical Accounts of Theory of Mind Development

Theoretical accounts of cognitive development typically fall into two broad categories: nativist and empiricist. Other ways to carve up theoretical accounts are domain-specific versus domain-general and one-system versus two-system accounts. The development of social cognition in general, and of ToM in particular, is also explained by such general frameworks. One of the first theoretical accounts of ToM was a nativist view based on research with children with ASD. According to that view, ToM has a specific innate basis in that the processes that determine the essential character of ToM do not apply to other cognitive domains and can be selectively impaired (Scholl & Leslie, 1999). Thus, the rapid, universal development of other people's mind understanding depends on an innate, encapsulated, and domain-specific part of the cognitive architecture, a Theory of Mind module (ToMM) (Baron-Cohen et al., 1985; Carruthers, 2002; Leslie, 1994). This view inspired researchers to conduct studies on children with autism who are high functioning to test if they display a ToM domain-specific delay or deficit (Baron-Cohen, 1995, 2000). For example, Poulin-Dubois and colleagues (2021) compared children with ASD to neurotypical children on tasks measuring naïve psychology, naïve physics, and naïve biology. Only children with ASD underperformed on an implicit false belief task (anticipatory looking paradigm), with performances in naïve biology and physics equivalent across the two groups and uncorrelated to performance on the false belief task. This result confirmed that naïve physics and biological reasoning are intact in children with ASD but that tracking false beliefs is challenging for this population. This view predicts that the acquisition of ToM should be largely uniform across individuals and cultures, although the timing of the acquisition might vary.

Another form of nativist account that is not based on modularity is the rich, mentalistic account of ToM development, which argues that false belief understanding emerges in infancy. For example, Baillargeon and colleagues (2010) favored a rich, mentalistic interpretation (see also Setoh et al., 2016) and claimed that false belief understanding is already present by the second year of life but is masked in traditional explicit tasks due to a number of executive task demands. First, children may lack sufficient skills at one of the processes involved in the task; for example, they may lack sufficient inhibitory-control skills to suppress their own knowledge or resist what is called the curse-of-knowledge – when knowledge of an event's outcome compromises the ability to reason about another person's beliefs about that event. Second, children may be able to execute each process separately but lack sufficient information-processing resources to handle the total concurrent processing demands of the task. This interpretation is supported by studies showing that performance on traditional false belied tasks (e.g., unexpected location change or content) improves when processing demands are reduced, even in toddlers (Scott, 2017; Scott & Baillargeon, 2017; Setoh et al., 2016). Similar to the mentalistic account of ToM development is the developmental enrichment account, which assumes that implicit false belief understanding develops into an explicit understanding through developing language and executive functions abilities. This account is supported by the link between implicit and explicit false belief understanding that has been reported in some longitudinal studies (Sodian et al., 2020).

Theoretical accounts of ToM development that focus on conceptual changes fall under the "constructivist" perspective. A theoretical account of ToM development that stands in contrast to the nativist modular view is so-called theory theory (Wellman, 1990, 2014). According to this constructivist, domain-specific view, scientific theories carve the world into different domains of knowledge, as is the case for naïve or folk theories, such as naïve psychology and naïve physics. The theory "predicts the three empirical signatures of constructivist learning: a) learning progresses in orderly conceptual steps, b) both the sequence and timetable of these steps depend on experience, c) prior conceptual knowledge constraints the development of each new step" (Wellman, 2014, p. 159). Another early account of ToM development that is also constructivist and domain-specific is the simulation theory (Goldman, 1992; Harris, 1992, 2000). According to the simulation approach, we have privileged access to our own mental states. This approach suggests that we adopt the perspective of others through simulation, hypothesizing their mental states based on our own experiences. For example, we may predict how someone else will respond to an emotion-arousing stimulus by imagining how we ourselves would respond. Or we may make sense of someone else's behavior by imagining what would lead us to behave in a similar way. Clearly, such ability depends on a capacity for imaginative pretense. Fortunately, in simulation theory such a capacity develops early in development – even 2- and 3-year-olds are remarkably skilled at pretense (Harris, 1992). However, pretense abilities improve with age, and such improvements contribute to developmental changes in ToM. To explain the sequence in the development of mental states, such as shown by the ToM scale, it is proposed that there are levels of difficulty in carrying out simulations for different mental states. Thus, some developments (e.g., reasoning about beliefs) are slower to emerge in childhood than others (e.g., reasoning about desires). The link between social pretense and performance on ToM tasks has been confirmed (Astington & Jenkins, 1995; Lohman & Tomasello, 2003). Additional evidence for this view comes from analyses of mental state language which show that children almost always make assertions about *want*, *know*, and *think* that are first focused on themselves (Harris et al., 2017).

Other theoretical views that can be classified as constructivist and psychosocial (à la Bronfenbrenner) also posit that a fundamental change occurs in ToM development around 4 years of age. Implicit false belief tasks may be passed by reliance on behavior rules (Perner & Ruffman, 2005) or other low-level processes (perceptual novelty; Heyes, 2014; statistical learning; Ruffman, 2014). In line with the bioecological theoretical framework, a full-fledged Theory of Mind emerges out of interactions with the proximal and distal social environment, with exposure to mental state talk and regularities in people's behavior as precursors (Ruffman, 2023). Only a few studies have directly tested these minimalist accounts of the evidence for early forms of ToM skills. As discussed earlier, in a study attempting to directly test the perceptual novelty account, Zmyj and colleagues (2015) found no link between a working memory test (A-not-B task) and false belief understanding (anticipatory looking task). Yott and Poulin-Dubois (2012) tested whether teaching infants a new rule might affect their reasoning on a false belief task. They taught 18-month-old infants over 8 trials that an object placed in one container always reappeared in a different container. They then examined whether learning this new rule affected infants' reasoning on a false belief task by making infants expect that the agent will search at the new location in the violation of expectation paradigm (i.e., show surprise when the agent searches at the old location). The researchers found no effect of training, which is inconsistent with the idea that infants use simple rules to succeed on implicit false belief tasks. If infants were processing false belief scenarios on learned behavioral rules (e.g., people always search for an object where they last saw it), they would have shown the opposite behavior at the test after learning that people never search at the last location. However, training might have been insufficient to overwrite the well-learned rule that people search for objects in the last place they saw them. (As discussed in the section on the stability of ToM, a link has been established between exposure to repeated behaviors and later mental state language; Ruffman et al., 2023.)

A two-system account of belief-ascription was put forward by Apperly and Butterfill (Apperly & Butterfill, 2009; Butterfill & Apperly, 2013; Low et al., 2016). There are two systems involved in understanding others' beliefs: a fast but inflexible one (Type 1) and a later-emerging more flexible one (Type 2). According to this view, the spontaneous responses in false belief tasks come from the Type 1 system, which helps us think about basic belief-like states called "registrations," but only in certain situations. The Type 2 system develops later, is flexible, and supports the attribution of genuine beliefs. This system is effortful and explicit but also inefficient and supports children's success in explicit false belief tasks. Such a flexible system allows children to overcome limitations posed by the early system and track more complex beliefs. Such a two-system account has been proposed to explain the apparent discrepancy between infants' early success in nonverbal mindreading tasks, on the one hand, and failures of children younger than 4 to pass verbally mediated false belief tasks, on the other. It assumes that two types of ToM develop independently. Type I ToM system operates implicitly and unconsciously and remains functional throughout the lifespan in the context of spontaneous-response tasks such as violation of expectation and anticipatory looking. Type II ToM – representational ToM – develops later, requires the development of language and executive function capacities, and operates in explicit and conscious ways across the lifespan. As discussed earlier, findings with infants and adults that show some dissociations between implicit and explicit tasks provide evidence for this dual process framework (Edwards & Low, 2017; Grosse Wiesmann et al., 2017; Low & Watts, 2013).

Another theory for the dissociation between the implicit and explicit ToM is the altercentric viewpoint developed by Southgate and colleagues (Kampis & Southgate, 2020; Southgate, 2020). An altercentric bias results from focusing on what others see or think, especially in the absence of a concept of self. Once one has developed one's own perspective, it can create a conflict when reasoning about false beliefs that requires executive functions, such as inhibitory control, to overcome. Thus, infants' apparent success in ToM tasks that require mature executive functions (which are sometimes challenging to adults) could be explained by the fact that they have an altercentric bias. A self-perspective emerges with the development of cognitive self-awareness sometime in the second year of life, at which point it leads to competition between one's own perspective and that of others. For example, in the seminal violation of expectation paradigm, the infant encodes that the agent witnesses a toy moving into the yellow box and maintains the agent's perspective despite the fact that the infant later sees that the toy moves to the green box, an event that would not be encoded with the same representational strength because it is not co-witnessed by another agent (Southgate, 2020). As a consequence, infants would correctly predict the agent to search in the yellow box in line with the agent's beliefs, although this would not entail that the infant represents this as the other's belief. The altercentric account thus predicts infants' surprise when an agent acts in a belief-incongruent way, explaining data from violation of expectation false belief tasks. In a similar way, encoding the agent's, rather than their own perspective, predicts infants' correct anticipation in previous anticipatory looking studies (e.g., Southgate et al., 2007) and their correct interpretation of others' communication and action prediction in interaction-based studies (e.g., Knudsen & Liszkowski, 2011; Southgate et al., 2010).

In summary, several theoretical accounts have been proposed to explain Theory of Mind development (see Ruffman, 2023, for a review of the main accounts). They all share the view that what allow the changes in ToM from infancy to preschool years are cognitive (e.g., executive functions, language) and social (e.g., social interactions) achievements. They diverge on the initial ToM competences that children initially possess, ranging from an implicit understanding of mental states to the detection of regularities in behaviors. After decades of research, is there an account that is most robustly supported by the data? Each theory is consistent with some research findings, although there is inconsistency in the findings linked to each account, as illustrated by the conflicting results of studies on the stability of Theory of Mind. Two environmental factors (repeated behaviors and maternal talk) and two developing insights (a sense of self and language) likely help children transition from an understanding of behavior to a ToM. To test the minimalist account's hypothesis that the foundations of Theory of Mind are parsimonious domain-general mechanisms, future research should adopt designs that expose infants to behavioral regularities and examine their impact on later Theory of Mind. Similarly, the impact of increased exposure to maternal talk on ToM development should be investigated. With regard to the rich, mentalist account is the wonder if it is falsifiable. Additional conceptual replications of implicit Theory of Mind tasks must be conducted to assess the depth of infants' reasoning in implicit ToM tasks. For example, infants' failure to infer false belief in the VOE paradigm when the agent turns her back or wears a veil when the object changes location provides key information about the fragility of ToM understanding in infancy (Poulin-Dubois et al., 2020).

5 Neural Foundations of Theory of Mind Development

Regardless of the theoretical perspective that one adopts, a consensus exists that neural changes support ToM development in addition to the cognitive and social correlates discussed earlier. Frith and Frith (1999) described the first major efforts to document neural bases of mentalizing. Their studies were conducted with positron emission tomography (PET), where the brains of small samples of adults were scanned while reading stories, which required either mental state reasoning (e.g., false beliefs) or physical state reasoning (Fletcher et al., 1995). They revealed a set of brain regions that were activated when people had to reason about mental states: in particular the medial prefrontal cortex (mPFC), superior posterior temporal sulcus (pSTS), and posterior cingulate cortex (PCC). Remarkably, this network of regions has been repeatedly identified in studies of mentalizing and is sometimes loosely referred to as the "social brain." In a review, Frith and Frith (2021) reported the progress in mapping the brain areas involved in ToM.

The neuroscience of ToM has contributed to clarifying the dissociation between implicit and explicit mentalizing. If the two types of tasks measure similar cognitive processes, similar brain regions should be implicated in their development. In contrast, if different brain regions are involved in successful performance on these tasks, this provides critical evidence for distinct underlying cognitive processes. Furthermore, a comparison of the relevant brain regions observed in children to those involved in ToM in adults would help identify which of these processes reflect mature ToM reasoning. Verbal, explicit ToM reasoning recruits a consistent network of brain regions, including the temporoparietal junction (TPJ), middle temporal gyrus (MTG), precuneus (PC), and medial prefrontal cortex in both adults (Schurz et al., 2014) and children (Grosse Wiesmann et al., 2017; Liu et al., 2008; Richardson et al., 2018; Saxe et al., 2009). This brain network shows increased connectivity, both functional and structural, at the age that children pass explicit ToM tasks. In contrast, research on the neural structures involved in implicit ToM tasks is scarce. Which brain regions underlie young children's success in implicit ToM tasks, and are they the same or different from those involved in the explicit ToM tasks? To address this issue, Grosse Wiesmann and colleagues (2020) tested children with MRI and a battery of implicit and explicit ToM tasks at the critical age of 3–4 years, corresponding to a developmental period before and after explicit ToM reasoning emerges. Markers of cortical brain structure (i.e., cortical thickness and surface area) were related to children's performance in novel nonverbal and traditional verbal ToM tasks. Explicit ToM reasoning was supported by cortical surface area and thickness of the precuneus and temporoparietal junction, which are brain areas typically involved in ToM in adults. In contrast, implicit ToM reasoning was supported by the cortical structure of an independent neural network, including the supramarginal gyrus. This double neural dissociation was also independent of other cognitive domains (language, executive function, general intelligence), providing strong support for two systems for reasoning about mental states – an explicit, verbal ToM that emerges around 4 years of age and an implicit nonverbal earlier-developing ToM (see Figure 6).

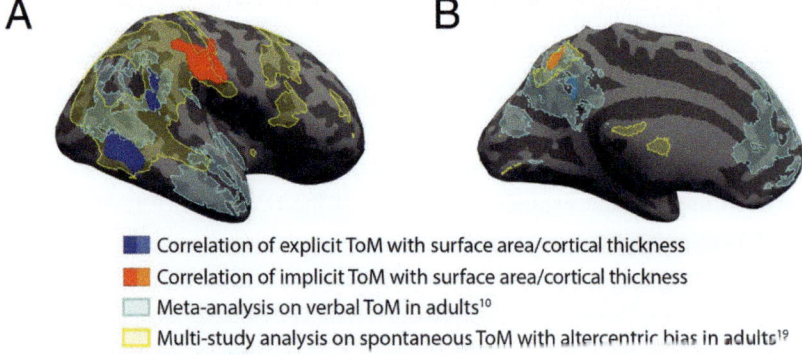

■ Correlation of explicit ToM with surface area/cortical thickness
■ Correlation of implicit ToM with surface area/cortical thickness
□ Meta-analysis on verbal ToM in adults[10]
□ Multi-study analysis on spontaneous ToM with altercentric bias in adults[19]

Figure 6 Distinct and independent brain regions associated with success on explicit (blue) and implicit ToM tasks (red, orange) for surface area (A) and cortical thickness (B) (figure reproduced from Grosse Wiesmann et al., 2020 with permission).

Regarding brain imaging research with even younger children, one study has used fNIRS to test the specific hypothesis that RTPJ is preferentially activated when young infants are reasoning about other people's mental states (Hyde et al., 2018). A replication of the false belief test based on the violation of expectation procedure with 7-month-olds was conducted (Onishi & Baillargeon, 2005). Participants watched a protagonist place an object in a container, leave, and then return to retrieve the object. As in the original VOE procedure, the object's location was changed during the induction trial when the protagonist was absent. Hyde and colleagues (2018) reported that the RTPJ showed increased blood oxygenation in adult participants, specifically when the target with the false belief returned to retrieve the object, compared to control conditions that did not involve a false belief. They observed a similar response in 7-month-old infants to that observed in adults: preferential increases in oxygenated blood over the RTPJ, specifically when the protagonist returned to search for the object. An fMRI study tested the link between neural development and behavioral changes in reasoning about others' minds by 4 to 5 years (Richardson et al., 2018). Children aged 3–12 years and adults watched a short movie while undergoing fMRI. The movie highlighted the characters' bodily sensations (often pain) and mental states (beliefs, desires, emotions). There were three main findings: (1) ToM and pain networks are functionally distinct by age 3 years, (2) functional specialization increases throughout childhood, and (3) functional maturity of each network is related to increasingly anti-correlated responses between the networks. Furthermore, the most studied milestone in ToM development, passing explicit false belief tasks, did not correspond to discontinuities in the development of the social brain. When it comes to the neural underpinnings of ToM achievements linked to emotion, a review by Bachmann et al. (2018) reports that emotional stimuli evoke greater neural responses than neutral stimuli and that the brain regions observed to have a significant activation during emotional processing encompass the action observation network (formed by the inferior frontal gyrus, the premotor cortex, and the inferior parietal lobe) and the mentalizing network (the temporoparietal junction, the temporal pole, the lateral orbitofrontal cortex, and the dorsomedial prefrontal cortex), making it possible for the individual to infer the other's emotions as mental states (Frith & Frith., 2006).

In summary, more research on the overlap in brain areas involved in ToM reasoning across ages is needed. Furthermore, future research will need to directly contrast brain activation during ToM tasks with activation involved during other social-cognitive processes in infants and young children. According to Grosse-Wiesmann et al. (2020, p. 6932), this remains a challenge as "it requires task-based functional MRI with very young children because the relatively low spatial resolution of infant neuroimaging methods (such as fNIRS) does not allow reliably measuring and dissociating the relevant brain regions (i.e., TPJ versus SMG and different portions of the PC)." Despite these challenges, understanding the neural processes underlying performance on implicit ToM success and their exact function must remain an approach in acquiring a better understanding of ToM development. Neuroscience could be a particularly useful tool to document Theory of Mind in infancy, and infant cognition in general, given that the behavioral measures used with infants are difficult to interpret and have weak psychometric properties (Turk-Browne & Aslin, 2024). This is well illustrated in a recent longitudinal study that examined the relationship between functional sensitivity of the right temporal-parietal junction (TPJ) to mental state processing in 7-month-old infants (as measured with the anticipatory looking paradigm) and explicit Theory of Mind reasoning in the same group several years later (Liu et al., 2025). Recall that TPJ is the brain region known to underlie Theory of Mind in older children and adults. Unexpectedly, the link was not between infant's brain activity during false belief processing but during a direct perception condition (false belief condition but with transparent boxes so the agent could see the new location of the object). Such evidence of a longitudinal brain-behavioral link from infancy to childhood provides support for stability of Theory of Mind across development, specifically between the understanding of seeing = knowing and later Theory of Mind. Thus, infant neuroscience provides a valuable contribution to the science of Theory of Mind development.

6 Summary and Future Directions

Now thousands of articles and books have been published on ToM, spanning the development of ToM across the lifespan. The universality of ToM and its evolutionary roots are also well documented, as is individual variability in reaching ToM milestones. We have seen that such variability has triggered a large body of work on the antecedents and correlates of Theory of Mind competence, including having siblings, engaging in conversations, and growing up bilingual. In addition, research has revealed the neural underpinnings of ToM, showing that different brain regions in the so-called ToM network are activated at different developmental stages, reflecting changes in the way ToM is used across the lifespan (Bowman & Wellman, 2014). To fully document ToM across the lifespan, a large number of measures have been developed over the years that assess the whole range of Theory of Mind constructs (for a review of adult measures, see Quesque & Rossetti, 2020, and Yeung et al., 2024; for measures for children, see Beaudoin et al., 2020, and Osterhaus & Bosacki,

2022). A large literature has also documented how ToM is relevant in other aspects of child development, such as pretend play, lying, academic achievement, and peer relationships.

This Element provides a review of the research on children's ToM that is necessarily selective, given the scope of the literature. This Element strives to balance breadth and depth, and the review reports interpretations that researchers offer for their findings and only occasionally critiques those findings. All studies have limitations, leaving their findings open to alternative explanations. Thus, the conclusions that are offered here are tentative until more research confirms these findings through new designs as well as strict and conceptual replications. As is typical with areas in which a large number of researchers explore a topic from different vantage points, variability across studies makes the comparison of findings challenging.

Given the scope of extant research on ToM, what future directions will this well-researched topic take? Despite progress made in better understanding this foundational ability, many aspects of ToM development and its determinants are still not well understood. First, the nature of ToM in infancy remains uncertain. The internal and external validity of all implicit ToM tasks remain to be demonstrated, casting doubt on whether there is a precocious form of advanced mindreading (e.g., false belief) in infancy that is implicit and unconscious (Poulin-Dubois et al., 2018). Indeed, the collective effort of the ManyBabies consortium in which the authors of original and replication studies test whether implicit ToM tasks are replicable across laboratories is an important step to address that issue (Schuwerk et al., 2025). More longitudinal studies will also need to be conducted with a wide range of ToM tasks both in infancy and in childhood. Importantly, control tasks that assess cognitive skills unrelated to ToM will be required to establish conceptual continuity of ToM. Nonetheless, it is important to note that evidence for stability does not provide conclusive proof for a full-fledged ToM in infancy but at least shows that implicit tasks measure abilities that are the building blocks for Theory of Mind development (Tomasello, 2018).

Among the promising avenues to clarify the status of infants' behaviors in implicit ToM tasks is the altercentric theoretical proposal (Grosse Wiesmann & Southgate, 2021; Kampis & Southgate, 2020; Southgate, 2020). Altercentrism in human cognition reflects that people's behaviors are spontaneously influenced by the presence and perspective of others, even when the task requires them to focus on their own point of view (Elekes et al., 2017; Kovács et al., 2010; Samson et al., 2010). Although this altercentric influence has been well studied in adults, there is little research on its developmental origins. According to this view, when an agent with a diverging perspective is present, infants' representation is impacted by the agent's perception of the situation, which means that infants do not focus on their own representation of the situation but simply encode events that are witnessed in common with another agent. This stronger encoding when another agent is present entails that infants will update their representation only when a change occurs that is witnessed together with the agent. In contrast, if a change occurs in the absence of the agent, infants will not update the representation that they encoded together with the agent. This would allow infants to make correct action predictions in line with the agent's belief without having to hold two conflicting perspectives. Before the development of a concept of self and with low executive functions, the altercentric bias might be an effective mechanism, which in most cases generates correct predictions while avoiding the complex cognitive demands of meta-representation. Support for this view is emerging. It remains to be seen how infants' predictions change as a function of self-concept development, as measured by tasks such as the mirror recognition test (see Calmette & Meunier, 2024, for a review of self-awareness and Theory of Mind).

A second line of research that requires attention concerns how children's Theory of Mind skills are expressed as a function of the characteristics of the agent. Infants appear to attribute mental states to any agents, with agents being defined as objects with a stable disposition to display mechanical (e.g., autonomous motion) and actional properties (i.e., goal-oriented, contingent, reactive-at-a-distance behavior) (Carey, 2009; Csibra, 2008; Leslie, 1994; Scholl & Tremoulet, 2000; Surian & Caldi, 2010). Thus, infants presented with chasing triangles, blobs, or mechanical cranes anticipate the actions of those agents consistently with their mental states (Burnside et al., 2020; Surian & Franchin, 2020; Surian & Geraci, 2012). Although the assumption that behaviors in implicit tasks reflect a rich Theory of Mind is contentious, the developmental progression of ToM reasoning across a wide range of agents remains to be more fully explored. A first wave of studies has used interviews as the main method and animals, plants, and artifacts as agents (for a review, see Goldman & Poulin-Dubois, 2024). ToM reasoning with social robots has gained attention, as robots allow for the manipulation of morphological features and dynamic cues (for reviews, see Stower et al., 2021; Marchetti et al., 2018). There is some evidence that younger children tend to anthropomorphize more than older children but that they attribute fewer mental states to robots than humans (Goldman et al., 2023; Manzi et al., 2020). An important step would be to test ToM with robots using scenarios such as those in the Wellman and Liu scale.

Yet another promising avenue of research is computer modeling. In order to confirm the causal role of many of the determinants of ToM, experimental studies are not ethically possible. For example, social interactions have been identified as impacting Theory of Mind development, as suggested by slower ToM in deaf children deprived of sign language, children with fewer siblings, and so on. Also, a comprehensive review of how child-level social tendencies can shape ToM showed that children's tendencies to attend to social information and engage in social interaction both played critical roles in Theory of Mind development (Lane & Bowman, 2021). To shed light on social interactions and ToM, Yu and Wellman (2023) conducted a computational experiment using agent-based modeling. They simulated agents (hypothetically, children) and assigned them to 10 groups, with a different amount of social interaction assigned to each group, from 1 to 10. In each group, agents randomly encountered one another and then interacted. The amount of social interaction strongly influenced how fast agents developed ToM, where more social interactions led to more rapid development. They also explored how other factors – such as having a prior, established social network or agents' network centrality – could influence the social interaction–ToM link. Then, they tested the model against real-world data from 84 deaf children and showed that the modeling results could explain the social interaction–ToM link observed in deaf children.

7 Conclusions

In the introduction to this Element, I wrote that I aimed to answer four central questions about the development of a Theory of Mind: What, When, Why, and How? The large body of work reviewed provides some answers to these questions. Concerning the *What* question, the key constructs of a Theory of Mind are now well known, and there is a consensus that there is a progression in the complexity of mental constructs that children develop over the first few years of life, from simple mental states such as goals to complex constructs such as second-order false belief. The dominant approach to measure preschoolers' understanding of these concepts has been through everyday scenarios enacted with props (Wellman & Liu, 2004). There is also effort devoted to measuring these constructs through parental reports, such as the Children's Social Understanding Scale, which appears to have good validity (Tahiroglu et al., 2014). Adaptations in a wide range of languages are desirable so that populations around the globe can be assessed, but whether it can substitute for laboratory-based tasks when relating ToM to other cognitive abilities remains to be clarified.

The *When* question remains one of the most contentious issues in the Theory of Mind literature. How rich is the reasoning that preverbal infants need to solve some implicit ToM tasks? Clearly, more cross-sectional and longitudinal research is needed once the validity and reliability of implicit tasks are established. New behavioral and neurological methodological approaches should also be developed. Nonetheless, building blocks are in place in infancy, including some core knowledge about agents, that provide the foundations for Theory of Mind development. These building blocks include joint attention, statistical learning, and inferential abilities that are the starting points of a cascade of more advanced socio-cognitive skills, including Theory of Mind.

Why is it important to study ToM development? We hope to have convinced the reader that deficits in ToM have negative consequences in other developmental domains: ToM abilities are associated with social skills (e.g., Banerjee & Yuill, 1999; Cassidy et al., 1992; Slaughter et al., 2002; Watson et al., 1999), and = academic performance (e.g., Doudin et al., 2001; Jones et al., 2011; Lecce et al., 2011). Given that ToM procedures have been found to be effective in improving children's ToM skills, past and future studies on ToM will benefit children by offering them the possibility to reach their full potential in domains known to impact their well-being across the lifespan (Hofmann et al., 2016).

Finally, the *How* question has received much attention from researchers over the past decades. Exciting new techniques, such as computer simulations, are starting to validate the main conclusions from behavioral studies. What remains to be clarified are the specific mechanisms involved in ToM. For example, there is solid empirical evidence that executive function and language both play crucial roles in acquiring metarepresentation. However, it is still unclear what underlying proximal mechanisms permit executive function and language to make metarepresentation possible. Continued research on the development of a ToM will enable a better understanding of how children explain and predict people's behaviors by inferring mental states and how such foundational skills could be supported to reach their optimal level.

Theory of Mind is the capacity for people to understand others and themselves as sentient agents with subjective perspectives on the world who act based on their mental states. This foundational form of social cognition rests on the ability to form metarepresentations, that is, having beliefs about others' beliefs. Although some primitive forms of ToM are evolutionarily ancient, are ontogenetically precocious, and appear to be shared with non-human primates, a mature, full-fledged metarepresentational ToM develops gradually over childhood. There appear to be milestones in ToM capacity during the second year of life and around 4 years of age. General neurocognitive capacities such as executive function and linguistic experience seem to facilitate that development, as well as a wide range of other social determinants, with many social and educational consequences. Still many key aspects of ToM development and its underpinnings are still poorly understood. For example, what mechanisms allow metarepresentation to emerge through executive function and language remain to be identified. The current debate concerning the role of language in ToM research should, therefore, be part of a much broader research program that aims to understand how language shapes thought during development. Likewise, the neural underpinnings of adult ToM are well documented, and studies are underway to reveal those relevant to developmental change. Future research will need to aim at developmental implementation theories, which detail how neural changes implement or realize cognitive transitions. New computational theories of the underpinnings of ToM (Baker et al., 2017; Jara-Ettinger, 2019) might have a crucial role in this endeavor. Finally, a central question for future study concerns the status of a nascent implicit ToM in infancy. Establishing the reliability and validity of implicit ToM tasks is underway as one of the projects of the ManyBabies consortium (Frank et al., 2017), a platform for replicability research in infant cognition. This consortium is currently testing whether the implicit ToM task based on anticipatory looking is replicable across laboratories (Schuwerk et al., 2025). Needless to say, even if this effort of replicability is successful, it will be insufficient in reaching a consensus about the richness of infants' reasoning. More conceptual replications of original studies as well as new experimental procedures are needed to clarify the richness and limitations of Theory of Mind during the first 2 years of life. The basic, theoretical question of the developmental origins of this foundational form of human social cognition could have practical applications, including the design of intervention programs that foster the development of social skills.

References

Adrián, J. E., Clemente, R. A., Villanueva, L., & Rieffe, C. (2005). Parent–child picture-book reading, Mothers' Mental State Language and children's Theory of Mind. *Journal of Child Language*, 32(3), 673–686. https://doi.org/10.1017/S0305000905006963.

Adrián, J. E., Clemente, R. A., & Villanueva, L. (2007). Mothers' use of cognitive state verbs in picture-book reading and the development of children's understanding of mind: A longitudinal study. *Child Development*, 78(4), 1052–1067. https://doi.org/10.1111/j.1467-8624.2007.01052.x.

Ainsworth, M. S., & Bowlby, J. (1991). An ethological approach to personality development. *American Psychologist*, 46(4), 333–341. https://doi.org/10.1037/0003-066X.46.4.333.

Aldrich, N. J., Chen, J., & Alfieri, L. (2021). Evaluating associations between parental mind-mindedness and children's developmental capacities through -analysis. *Developmental Review*, 60, 100946. https://doi.org/10.1016/j.dr.2021.100946.

Andrews, G., Halford, G. S., Bunch, K. M., Bowden, D., & Jones, T. (2003). Theory of mind and relational complexity. *Child Development*, 74(5), 1476–1499. https://doi.org/10.1111/1467-8624.00618.

Apperly, I. A., & Butterfill, S. A. (2009). Do humans have two systems to track beliefs and belief-like states? *Psychological Review*, 116(4), 953–970. https://doi.org/10.1037/a0016923.

Aschersleben, G., Hofer, T., & Jovanovic, B. (2008). The link between infant attention to goal-directed action and later Theory of Mind abilities. *Developmental Science*, 11(6), 862–868. https://doi.org/10.1111/j.1467-7687.2008.00736.x.

Astington, J. W. (1994). *The child's discovery of the mind*. Harvard University Press.

Astington, J. W., Harris, P. L., & Olson, D. R. (1988). *Developing theories of mind*. Cambridge University Press.

Astington, J. W., & Jenkins, J. M. (1995). Theory of Mind development and social understanding. *Cognition and Emotion*, 9(2-3), 151–165. https://doi.org/10.1080/02699939508409006.

Astington, J. W., & Jenkins, J. M. (1999). A longitudinal study of the relation between language and theory-of-mind development. *Developmental Psychology*, 35(5), 1311–1320. https://doi.org/10.1037/0012-1649.35.5.1311.

Austin, G., Groppe, K., & Elsner, B. (2014). The reciprocal relationship between executive function and Theory of Mind in middle childhood: A 1-year longitudinal perspective. *Frontiers in Psychology*, 5, 1–11. https://doi.org/10.3389/fpsyg.2014.00655.

Avis, J., & Harris, P. L. (1991). Belief-desire reasoning among Baka children: Evidence for a universal conception of mind. *Child Development*, 62(3), 460–467. https://doi.org/10.2307/1131123.

Babu, N., Khurana, R., & Lochan, A. (2023) The role of Theory of Mind, executive function and language on children's lying behaviour. *Journal of Cognitive Psychology*, 35(6-7), 650–662. https://doi.org/10.1080/20445911.2023.2244736.

Bachmann, J., Munzert, J., & Krüger, B. (2018). Neural underpinnings of the perception of emotional states derived from biological human motion: A review of neuroimaging research. *Frontiers in Psychology*, 9, 1763. https://doi.org/10.3389/fpsyg.2018.01763.

Baillargeon, R., Buttelmann, D., & Southgate, V. (2018). Invited commentary: Interpreting failed replications of early false-belief findings: Methodological and theoretical considerations. *Cognitive Development*, 46, 112–124. https://doi.org/10.1016/j.cogdev.2018.06.001.

Baillargeon, R., Scott, R. M., & He, Z. (2010). False-belief understanding in infants. *Trends in Cognitive Sciences*, 14(3), 110–118. https://doi.org/10.1016/j.tics.2009.12.006.

Baker, C. L., Jara-Ettinger, J., Saxe, R., & Tenenbaum, J. B. (2017). Rational quantitative attribution of beliefs, desires and percepts in human mentalizing. *Nature Human Behaviour*, 1(4). https://doi.org/10.1038/s41562-017-0064.

Banerjee, R., & Yuill, N. (1999). Children's explanations for self-presentational behaviour. *European Journal of Social Psychology*, 29(1), 105–111. https://doi.org/10.1002/(SICI)1099-0992(199902)29:1<105::AID-EJSP910>3.0.CO;2-K.

Baron-Cohen, S. (1995). *Mindblindness: An essay on autism and Theory of Mind*. MIT Press. https://doi.org/10.7551/mitpress/4635.001.0001.

Baron-Cohen, S. (2000). Theory of Mind and autism: A review. *Autism*, 23-(655), 169–184. https://doi.org/10.1016/S0074-7750(00)80010-5.

Baron-Cohen, S., Leslie, A. M., & Frith, U. (1985). Does the autistic child have a "Theory of Mind"? *Cognition*, 21(1), 37–46. https://doi.org/10.1016/0010-0277(85)90022-8.

Barone, P., Corradi, G., & Gomila, A. (2019). Infants' performance in spontaneous-response false belief tasks: A review and meta-analysis. *Infant Behavior and Development*, 57, 101350. https://doi.org/10.1016/j.infbeh.2019.101350.

References

Bartsch, K., & Wellman, H. M. (1995). *Children talk about the mind.* Oxford University Press. https://doi.org/10.1002/1520-6807(199601)33:1<87:: AID-PITS2310330105>3.0.CO;2-C.

Beaudoin, C., Leblanc, É., Gagner, C., & Beauchamp, M. H. (2020). Systematic review and inventory of Theory of Mind measures for young children. *Frontiers in Psychology*, 10(2905). https://doi.org/10.3389/fpsyg.2019.02905.

Benson, J. E., Sabbagh, M. A., Carlson, S. M., & Zelazo, P. D. (2013). Individual differences in executive functioning predict preschoolers' improvement from theory-of-mind training. *Developmental Psychology*, 49(9), 1615–1627. https://doi.org/10.1037/a0031056.

Białecka, M., Gut, A., Stępień-Nycz, M., Macheta, K., & Janczura, J. (2024). Beyond the false belief task: How children develop their knowledge about the mind. *Infant and Child Development*, 33(5), e2528. https://doi.org/10.1002/icd.2528.

Bialystok, E., & Senman, L. (2004). Executive processes in appearance-reality tasks: The role of inhibition of attention and symbolic representation. *Child Development*, 75(2), 562–579. https://doi.org/10.1111/j.1467-8624.2004.00693.x.

Bianco, F., Lecce, S., & Banerjee, R. (2016). Conversations about mental states and Theory of Mind development during middle childhood: A training study. *Journal of Experimental Child Psychology*, 149, 41–61. https://doi.org/10.1016/j.jecp.2015.11.006.

Birch, S. A. J., Li, V., Haddock, T. et al. (2017). Perspectives on perspective taking: How children think about the minds of others. In J. B. Benson, eds., *Advances in child development and behavior*. Academic Press, pp. 185–226. http://dx.doi.org/10.1016/bs.acdb.2016.10.005.

Bornstein, M. H., Putnick, D. L., & Esposito, G. (2017). Continuity and stability in development. *Child Dev Perspect*, 11(2), 113–119. https://doi.org/10.1111/cdep.12221.

Bowman, L. C., & Wellman, H. M. (2014). Neuroscience contributions to childhood theory of mind development. In O. N. Saracho, eds., *Contemporary Perspectives on Research in Theory of Mind in Early Childhood Education*. Information Age, pp. 195–223.

Brandone, A. C., & Stout, W. (2023). Mentalistic and normative frameworks in children's explanations of others' behaviors. *Child Development*, 95, e139–e154. https://doi.org/10.1111/cdev.14027.

Bretherton, I. (1985). Attachment theory: Retrospect and prospect. *Monographs of the Society for Research in Child Development*, 50(1-2), 3–35. https://doi.org/10.2307/3333824.

Bretherton, I. (1990). Open communication and internal working models: Their role in the development of attachment relationships. In R. A. Thompson, eds., *Nebraska Symposium on Motivation, 1988: Socioemotional development*. University of Nebraska Press, pp. 57–113.

Brink, K. A., Lane, J. D., & Wellman, H. M. (2015). Developmental Pathways for Social Understanding: Linking social cognition to social contexts. *Frontiers in Psychology*, 6(719). https://doi.org/10.3389/fpsyg.2015.00719.

Buac, M., & Kaushanskaya, M. (2020). Predictors of Theory of Mind performance in bilingual and monolingual children. *International Journal of Bilingualism*, 24(2), 339–359. https://doi.org/10.1177/1367006919826866.

Burnside, K., Neumann, C., & Poulin-Dubois, D. (2020). Infants generalize beliefs across individuals. *Frontiers in Psychology*, 11(547680). https://doi.org/10.3389/fpsyg.2020.547680.

Burnside, K., Severdija, V., & Poulin-Dubois, D. (2020). Infants attribute false beliefs to a toy crane. *Developmental Science*, 23(2), Article e12887. https://doi.org/10.1111/desc.12887.

Buttelmann, D., Carpenter, M., & Tomasello, M. (2009). Eighteen-month-old infants show false belief understanding in an active helping paradigm. *Cognition*, 112(2), 337–342. https://doi.org/10.1016/j.cognition.2009.05.006.

Butterfill, S. A., & Apperly, I. A. (2013). How to construct a minimal Theory of Mind. *Mind & Language*, 28(5), 606–637. https://doi.org/10.1111/mila.12036.

Byers-Heinlein, K., Bergmann, C., & Savalei, V. (2021). Six solutions for more reliable infant research. *Infant and Child Development*, 31(5), e2296. https://doi.org/10.1002/icd.2296.

Cahill, K. R., Deater-Deckard, K., Pike, A., & Hughes, C. (2007). Theory of Mind, self-worth and the mother–child relationship. *Social Development*, 16(1), 45–56. https://doi.org/10.1111/j.1467-9507.2007.00371.x.

Callaghan, T., Rochat, P., Lillard, A. et al. (2005). Synchrony in the onset of mental-state reasoning. *Psychological Science*, 16(5), 378–384. https://doi.org/10.1111/j.0956-7976.2005.01544.x.

Calmette, T., & Meunier, H. (2024). Is self-awareness necessary to have a Theory of Mind? *Biol Rev*, 99(5), 1736–1771. https://doi.org/10.1111/brv.13090.

Carey, S. (2009). *The origin of concepts*. Oxford University Press. https://doi.org/10.1093/acprof:oso/9780195367638.001.0001.

Carlson, S. M., Mandell, D. J., & Williams, L. (2004). Executive function and Theory of Mind: Stability and Prediction From Ages 2 to 3. *Developmental Psychology*, 40(6), 1105–1122. https://doi.org/10.1037/0012-1649.40.6.1105.

Carlson, S. M., & Moses, L. J. (2001). Individual differences in inhibitory control and children's Theory of Mind. *Child Development*, 72(4), 1032–1053. https://doi.org/10.1111/1467-8624.00333.

Carlson, S. M., Moses, L. J., & Breton, C. (2002). How specific is the relation between executive function and Theory of Mind? Contributions of inhibitory control and working memory. *Infant and Child Development*, 11(2), 73–92. https://doi.org/10.1002/icd.298.

Carlson, S. M., Moses, L. J., & Claxton, L. J. (2004). Individual differences in executive functioning and Theory of Mind: An investigation of inhibitory control and planning ability. *Journal of Experimental Child Psychology*, 87(4), 299–319. https://doi.org/10.1016/j.jecp.2004.01.002.

Carlson, S. M., Moses, L. J., & Hix, H. R. (1998). The role of inhibitory processes in young children's difficulties with deception and false belief. *Child Development*, 69(3), 672. https://doi.org/10.1111/j.1467-8624.1998.tb06236.x.

Carruthers, P. (2002). The cognitive functions of language. *Behavioral and Brain Sciences*, 25(6), 657–726. https://doi.org/10.1017/S0140525X02000122.

Cassidy, J., Parke, R. D., Butkovsky, L., & Braungart, J. M. (1992). Family-peer connections: The roles of emotional expressiveness within the family and children's understanding of emotions. *Child Development*, 63(3), 603–618. https://doi.org/10.2307/1131349.

Cheung, H., Mak, W. Y., Luo, X., & Xiao, W. (2010). Sociolinguistic awareness and false belief in young Cantonese learners of English. *Journal of Experimental Child Psychology*, 107(2), 188–194. https://doi.org/10.1016/j.jecp.2010.05.001.

Chiarella, S. S., & Poulin-Dubois, D. (2013). Cry babies and pollyannas: Infants can detect unjustified emotional reactions. *Infancy*, 18, E81–E96. https://doi.org/10.1111/infa.12028.

Clements, W. A., & Perner, J. (1994). Implicit understanding of belief. *Cognitive Development*, 9(4), 377–395. https://doi.org/10.1016/0885-2014(94)90012-4.

Cole, K., & Mitchell, P. (1998). Family background in relation to deceptive ability and understanding of the mind. *Social Development*, 7(2), 181–197. https://doi.org/10.1111/1467-9507.00061.

Cole, K., & Mitchell, P. (2000). Siblings in the development of executive control and a Theory of Mind. *British Journal of Developmental Psychology*, 18(2), 279–295. https://doi.org/10.1348/026151000165698.

Conger, R. D., & Donnellan, M. B. (2007). An interactionist perspective on the socioeconomic context of human development. *Annual Review of*

Psychology, 58, 175–199. https://doi.org/10.1146/annurev.psych.58.110405.085551.

Csibra, G. (2008). Goal attribution to inanimate agents by 6.5-month-old infants. *Cognition*, 107(2), 705–717. https://doi.org/10.1016/j.cognition.2007.08.001.

Cutting, A. L., & Dunn, J. (1999). Theory of Mind, emotion understanding, language, and family background: Individual differences and interrelations. *Child Development*, 70(4), 853–865. https://doi.org/10.1111/1467-8624.00061.

Dahlgren, S. O., Almén, H., & Dahlgren Sandberg, A. (2017). Theory of Mind and executive functions in young bilingual children. *Journal of Genetic Psychology*, 178(5), 303–307. https://doi.org/10.1080/00221325.2017.1361376.

de Rosnay, M., Pons, F., Harris, P. L., & Morrell, J. M. (2004). A lag between understanding false belief and emotion attribution in young children: Relationships with linguistic ability and mothers' mental-state language. *British Journal of Developmental Psychology*, 22(2), 197–218 https://doi.org/10.1348/026151004323044573.

de Villiers, J. G. (2007). The interface of language and Theory of Mind. *Lingua*, 117(11), 1858–1878. https://doi.org/10.1016/j.lingua.2006.11.006.

de Villiers, J. G., & Pyers, J. E. (2002). Complements to cognition: A longitudinal study of the relationship between complex syntax and false-belief-understanding. *Cognitive Development*, 17(1), 1037–1060. https://doi.org/10.1016/S0885-2014(02)00073-4.

de Villiers, J. G., & de Villiers, P. A. (2000). Linguistic determinism and the understanding of false beliefs. In P. Mitchell & K. J. Riggs, eds., *Children's reasoning and the mind*. Psychology Press/Taylor & Francis, pp. 191–228.

de Villiers, J., & de Villiers, P. (2009). Complements enable representation of the contents of false beliefs: The evolution of a Theory of Mind. In S. Foster, eds., *Language acquisition*. New York: Palgrave McMillian, pp. 169–195. https://doi.org/10.1057/9780230240780_8.

Demers, I., Bernier, A., Tarabulsy, G. M., & Provost, M. A. (2010). Maternal and child characteristics as antecedents of maternal mind-mindedness. *Infant Mental Health Journal*, 31(1), 94–112. https://doi.org/10.1002/imhj.20244.

Devine, R. T., & Apperly, I. A. (2022). Willing and able? Theory of Mind, social motivation, and social competence in middle childhood and early adolescence. *Developmental Science*, 25, e13137. https://doi.org/10.1111/desc.13137.

Devine, R. T., & Hughes, C. (2013). Silent Films and Strange Stories: Theory of Mind, gender, and social experiences in middle childhood. *Child Development*, 84(3), 989–1003. https://doi.org/10.1111/cdev.12017.

Devine, R. T., & Hughes, C. (2014). Relations between false belief understanding and executive function in early childhood: A meta-analysis. *Child Development*, 85(5), 1777–1794. https://doi.org/10.1111/cdev.12237.

Devine, R. T., & Hughes, C. (2018). Family correlates of false belief understanding in early childhood: A meta-analysis. *Child Development*, 89(3), 971–987. https://doi.org/10.1111/cdev.12682.

Devine, R. T., & Hughes, C. (2019). Let's talk: Parents' mental talk (not mind-mindedness or mindreading capacity) predicts children's false belief understanding. *Child Development*, 90(4), 1236–1253. https://doi.org/10.1111/cdev.12990.

Diamond, A. (2013). Executive functions. *Annual Review of Psychology*, 64(1), 135–168. https://doi.org/10.1146/annurev-psych-113011-143750.

Diaz, V., & Farrar, M. J. (2018a). The missing explanation of the false-belief advantage in bilingual children: A longitudinal study. *Developmental Science*, 21(4). https://doi.org/10.1111/desc.12594.

Diaz, V., & Farrar, M. J. (2018b). Do bilingual and monolingual preschoolers acquire false belief understanding similarly? The role of executive functioning and language. *First Language*, 38(4), 382–398. https://doi.org/10.1177/0142723717752741.

Doudin, P. A., Martin, D., & Albanese, O. (2001). *Metacognition et éducation: Théorie et pratique*. Peter Lang.

Duncan, G. J., & Magnuson, K. (2012). Socioeconomic status and cognitive functioning: Moving from correlation to causation. *WIREs Cognitive Science*, 3(3), 377–386. https://doi.org/10.1002/wcs.1176.

Dunn, J., Brown, J., Slomkowski, C., Tesla, C., & Youngblade, L. (1991). Young children's understanding of other people's feelings and beliefs: individual differences and their antecedents. *Child Development*, 62(6), 1352–1366. https://doi.org/10.1111/j.1467-8624.1991.tb01610.x.

Dunphy-Lelii, S., LaBounty, J., Lane, J. D., & Wellman, H. M. (2014). The social context of infant intention understanding. *Journal of Cognition and Development*, 15(1), 60–77. https://doi.org/10.1080/15248372.2012.710863.

Durrleman, S., Bentea, A., Prisecaru, A., Thommen, E., & Delage, H. (2022). Training syntax to enhance Theory of Mind in children with ASD. *Autism and Developmental Disorders*, 53(6), 2444–2457. https://doi.org/10.1007/s10803-022-05507-0.

Dykas, M. J., & Cassidy, J. (2011). Attachment and the processing of social information across the life span: Theory and evidence. *Psychological Bulletin*, 137(1), 19–46. https://doi.org/10.1037/a0021367.

Ebert, S., Peterson, C., Slaughter, V., & Weinert, S. (2017). Links among parents' mental state language, family socioeconomic status, and preschoolers' Theory of Mind development. *Cognitive Development*, 44, 32–48. https://doi.org/10.1016/j.cogdev.2017.08.005.

Edwards, K., & Low, J. (2017). Reaction time profiles of adults' action prediction reveal two mindreading systems. *Cognition*, 160, 1–16. https://doi.org/10.1016/j.cognition.2016.12.004.

Egyed, K., Király, I., & Gergely, G. (2013). Communicating shared knowledge in infancy. *Psychological Science*, 24(7), 1348–1353. https://doi.org/10.1177/0956797612471952.

Elekes, F., Varga, M., & Király, I. (2017). Level-2 perspectives computed quickly and spontaneously: Evidence from eight- to 9.5-year-Old children. *British Journal of Developmental Psychology*, 35(4), 609–622. https://doi.org/10.1111/bjdp.12201.

Ensor, R., & Hughes, C. (2008). Content or connectedness? Mother–child talk and early social understanding. *Child Development*, 79(1), 201–216. https://doi.org/10.1111/j.1467-8624.2007.01120.x.

Ereky-Stevens, K. (2008). Associations between mothers' sensitivity to their infants' internal states and children's later understanding of mind and emotion. *Infant and Child Development*, 17(5), 527–543. https://doi.org/10.1002/icd.572.

Fan, S. P., Liberman, Z., Keysar, B., & Kinzler, K. D. (2015). The exposure advantage. *Psychological Science*, 26(7), 1090–1097. https://doi.org/10.1177/0956797615574699.

Farah, M. J. (2017). The neuroscience of socioeconomic status: Correlates, causes, and consequences. *Neuron*, 96(1), 56–71. https://doi.org/10.1016/j.neuron.2017.08.034.

Farrant, B. M., Devine, T. A. J., Maybery, M. T., & Fletcher, J. (2012). Empathy, perspective taking and prosocial behaviour: The importance of parenting practices. *Infant and Child Development*, 21(2), 175–188. https://doi.org/10.1002/icd.740.

Farrar, M. J., & Maag, L. (2002). Early language development and the emergence of a Theory of Mind. *First Language*, 22(65, Pt2), 197–213. https://doi.org/10.1177/014272370202206504.

Fearon, R. P., Bakermans-Kranenburg, M. J., Van IJzendoorn, M. H., Lapsley, A., & Roisman, G. I. (2010). The significance of insecure attachment and disorganization in the development of children's externalizing behavior: A Meta-analytic study. *Child Development*, 81(2), 435–456. https://doi.org/10.1111/j.1467-8624.2009.01405.x.

Fink, E., Begeer, S., Peterson, C. C., Slaughter, V., & de Rosnay, M. (2015). Friendlessness and theory of mind: A prospective longitudinal study. *British Journal of Developmental Psychology*, 33(1), 1–17. https://doi.org/10.1111/bjdp.12060.

Flavell, J. H. (1968). *The development of role-taking and communication skills in children*. John Wiley & Sons.

Fletcher, P., Happé, F., Frith, U. et al. (1995). Other minds in the brain: A functional imaging study of "Theory of Mind" in story comprehension. *Cognition*, 57(2), 109–128. https://doi.org/10.1016/0010-0277(95)00692-R.

Flynn, E., O'Malley, C., & Wood, D. (2004). A longitudinal, microgenetic study of the emergence of false belief understanding and inhibition skills. *Developmental Science*, 7(1), 103–115. https://doi.org/10.1111/j.1467-7687.2004.00326.x.

Fonagy, P., Steele, M., Steele, H., Moran, G. S., & Higgitt, A. C. (1991). The capacity for understanding mental states: The reflective self in parent and child and its significance for security of Attachment. *Infant Mental Health Journal*, 12(3), 201–218. https://doi.org/10.1002/1097-0355(199123)12:3<201::AID-IMHJ2280120307>3.0.CO;2-7.

Frank, M. C., Bergelson, E., Bergmann, C. et al. (2017). A collaborative approach to infant research: Promoting reproducibility, best practices, and theory-building. *Infancy*, 22(4), 421–435. https://doi.org/10.1111/infa.12182.

Frith, C. D., & Frith, U. (1999). Interacting minds–a biological basis. *Science*, 286(5445), 1692–1695. https://doi.org/10.1126/science.286.5445.1692.

Frith, C. D., & Frith, U. (2006). The neural basis of mentalizing. *Neuron*, 50(4), 531–534. https://doi.org/10.1016/j.neuron.2006.05.001.

Frith, C. D., & Frith, U. (2021). Mapping mentalising in the brain. In M. Gilead & K. N. Ochsner, eds., *The neural basis of mentalizing*. Springer, Cham., pp. 17–45. https://doi.org/10.1007/978-3-030-51890-5_2.

Frye, D., David Zelazo, P., & Burack, J. A. (1998). Cognitive complexity and Control. *Current Directions in Psychological Science*, 7(4), 116–121. https://doi.org/10.1111/1467-8721.ep10774754.

Frye, D., Zelazo, P. D., & Palfai, T. (1995). Theory of Mind and rule-based reasoning. *Cognitive Development*, 10(4), 483–527. https://doi.org/10.1016/0885-2014(95)90024-1

Gariepy, J.-F., Watson, K. K., Du, E. et al. (2014). Social learning in humans and other animals. *Frontiers in Neuroscience*, 8(58). https://doi.org/10.3389/fnins.2014.00058.

Garon, N., Bryson, S. E., & Smith, I. M. (2008). Executive function in preschoolers: A review using an integrative framework. *Psychological Bulletin*, 134(1), 31–60. https://doi.org/10.1037/0033-2909.134.1.31.

Gilbert, D. T., King, G., Pettigrew, S., & Wilson, T. D. (2016). Comment on "estimating the reproducibility of psychological science." *Science*, 351(6277), 1037–1037. https://doi.org/10.1126/science.aad7243.

Goetz, P. J. (2003). The effects of bilingualism on Theory of Mind development. *Bilingualism: Language and Cognition*, 6(1), 1–15. https://doi.org/10.1017/S1366728903001007.

Goldman, A. I. (1992). In defense of the simulation theory. *Mind and Language*, 7(1–2), 104–119. https://doi.org/10.1111/j.1468-0017.1992.tb00200.x.

Goldman, E. J., Baumann, A.-E., & Poulin-Dubois, D. (2023). Preschoolers' anthropomorphizing of robots: Do human-like properties matter? *Frontiers in Psychology*, 13, 1102370. https://doi.org/10.3389/fpsyg.2022.1102370.

Goldman, E. J., & Poulin-Dubois, D. (2024). Children's anthropomorphism of inanimate agents. *WIREs Cognitive Science*, 15(4), e1676. https://doi.org/10.1002/wcs.1676.

Groh, A. M., Narayan, A. J., Bakermans-Kranenburg, M. J. et al. (2017). Attachment and temperament in the early life course: A meta-analytic review. *Child Development*, 88(3), 770–795. https://doi.org/10.1111/cdev.12677.

Grosse Wiesmann, C., Friederici, A. D., Disla, D., Steinbeis, N., & Singer, T. (2018). Longitudinal evidence for 4-year-olds' but not 2- and 3-year-olds' false belief-related action anticipation. *Cognitive Development*, 46, 58–68. https://doi.org/10.1016/j.cogdev.2017.08.007.

Grosse Wiesmann, C., Friederici, A. D., Singer, T., & Steinbeis, N. (2020). Two systems for thinking about others' thoughts in the developing brain. *Proceedings of the National Academy of Sciences*, 117(12), 6928–6935. https://doi.org/10.1073/pnas.1916725117.

Grosse Wiesmann, C., Schreiber, J., Singer, T., Steinbeis, N., & Friederici, A. D. (2017). White matter maturation is associated with the emergence of Theory of Mind in early childhood. *Nature Communications*, 8(1). https://doi.org/10.1038/ncomms14692.

Grosse Wiesmann, C., & Southgate, V. (2021). Early theory of mind development: Are infants inherently altercentric? In K. N. Ochsner & M. Gilead, eds., *The Neural Basis of Mentalizing*. Springer, Cham., pp. 49–66. https://doi.org/10.1007/978-3-030-51890-5_3.

Guajardo, N. R., Snyder, G., & Petersen, R. (2009). Relationships among parenting practices, parental stress, child behaviour, and children's social-cognitive development. *Infant and Child Development*, 18(1), 37–60. https://doi.org/10.1002/icd.578.

Hackman, D. A., & Farah, M. J. (2009). Socioeconomic status and the developing brain. *Trends in Cognitive Sciences*, 13(2), 65–73. https://doi.org/10.1016/j.tics.2008.11.003.

Hala, S., Hug, S., & Henderson, A. (2003). Executive function and false-belief understanding in Preschool children: Two tasks are harder than one. *Journal of Cognition and Development*, 4(3), 275–298. https://doi.org/10.1207/S15327647JCD0403_03.

Hale, C. M., & Tager-Flusberg, H. (2003). The influence of language on Theory of Mind: A training study. *Developmental Science*, 6(3), 346–359. https://doi.org/10.1111/1467-7687.00289.

Harris, P. L. (1992). From simulation to folk psychology: The case for development. *Mind & Language*, 7(1-2), 120–144. https://doi.org/10.1111/j.1468-0017.1992.tb00201.x.

Harris, P. L. (2000). *The work of the imagination*. Malden, MA: Blackwell.

Harris, P. L., Yang, B., & Cui, Y. (2017). 'I don't know': Children's early talk about knowledge. *Mind and Language*, 32(3), 283–307. https://doi.org/10.1111/mila.12143.

Heider, F., & Simmel, M. (1944). An experimental study of apparent behavior. *The American Journal of Psychology*, 57, 243–259. https://doi.org/10.2307/1416950.

Heyes, C. (2014). False belief in infancy: A fresh look. *Developmental Science*, 17(5), 647–659. https://doi.org/10.1111/desc.12148.

Hofmann, S. G., Doan, S. N., Sprung, M. et al. (2016). Training children's theory-of-mind: A meta-analysis of controlled studies. *Cognition*, 150, 200–212. https://doi.org/10.1016/j.cognition.2016.01.006.

Holmes-Lonergan, H. A. (2003). Understanding of affective false beliefs, perceptions of parental discipline, and classroom behavior in children from Head Start. *Early Education and Development*, 14(1), 29–46. https://doi.org/10.1207/s15566935eed1401_3.

Howe, N., Petrakos, H., & Rinaldi, C. M. (1998). "All the sheeps are dead. He murdered them": Sibling pretense, negotiation, internal state language, and relationship quality. *Child Development*, 69(1), 182–191. https://doi.org/10.2307/1132079.

Howe, N., Rinaldi, C. M., Jennings, M., & Petrakos, H. (2002). "No! The lambs can stay out because they got cozies!": Constructive and destructive sibling conflict, pretend play, and social understanding. *Child Development*, 73(5), 1460–1473. https://doi.org/10.1111/1467-8624.00483.

Hughes, C. (1998). Executive function in preschoolers: Links with Theory of Mind and verbal ability. *British Journal of Developmental Psychology*, 16(2), 233–253. https://doi.org/10.1111/j.2044-835X.1998.tb00921.x.

Hughes, C. (2011). *Social understanding and social lives: From toddlerhood through to the transition to school*. New York: Psychology Press. https://doi.org/10.1002/icd.760.

Hughes, C., Deater-Deckard, K., & Cutting, A. L. (1999). "Speak roughly to your little boy?" Sex differences in the relations between parenting and preschoolers' understanding of mind. *Social Development*, 8(2), 143–160. https://doi.org/10.1111/1467-9507.00088.

Hughes, C., & Devine, R. T. (2015). Individual differences in theory of mind from Preschool to Adolescence: Achievements and directions. *Child Dev Perspect*, 9, 149–153. https://doi.org/10.1111/cdep.12124.

Hughes, C., Dunn, J., & White, A. (1998). Trick or treat? Uneven understanding of mind and emotion and executive dysfunction in "hard-to-manage" preschoolers. *Journal of Child Psychology and Psychiatry*, 39(7), 981–994. https://doi.org/10.1111/1469-7610.00401.

Hughes, C., & Ensor, R. (2005). Executive function and theory of mind in 2 year olds: A family affair? *Developmental Neuropsychology*, 28(2), 645–668. https://doi.org/10.1207/s15326942dn2802_5.

Hughes, C., & Ensor, R. (2006). Behavioural problems in 2-year-olds: Links with individual differences in Theory of Mind, executive function and harsh parenting. *Journal of Child Psychology and Psychiatry*, 47(5), 488–497. https://doi.org/10.1111/j.1469-7610.2005.01519.x.

Hughes, C., & Ensor, R. (2007). Executive function and Theory of Mind: Predictive relations from ages 2 to 4. *Developmental Psychology*, 43(6), 1447–1459. https://doi.org/10.1037/0012-1649.43.6.1447.

Hyde, D. C., Simon, C. E., Ting, F., & Nikolaeva, J. I. (2018). Functional organization of the temporal–parietal junction for Theory of Mind in preverbal infants: A near-infrared spectroscopy study. *The Journal of Neuroscience*, 38(18), 4264–4274. https://doi.org/10.1523/JNEUROSCI.0264-17.2018.

Imuta, K., Henry, J. D., Slaughter, V., Selcuk, B., & Ruffman, T. (2016). Theory of Mind and prosocial behavior in childhood: A meta-analytic review. *Developmental Psychology*, 52(8), 1192–1205. https://doi.org/10.1037/dev0000140.

Jara-Ettinger, J. (2019). Theory of Mind as inverse reinforcement learning. *Current Opinion in Behavioral Sciences*, 29, 105–110. https://doi.org/10.1016/j.cobeha.2019.04.010.

Jenkins, J. M., & Astington, J. W. (1996). Cognitive factors and family structure associated with Theory of Mind development in young children. *Developmental Psychology*, 32(1), 70–78. https://doi.org/10.1037/0012-1649.32.1.70.

Jones, C. R., Simonoff, E., Baird, G. et al. (2017). The association between Theory of Mind, executive function, and the symptoms of autism spectrum disorder. *Autism Research*, 11(1), 95–109. https://doi.org/10.1002/aur.1873.

Jones, S. M., Brown, J. L., & Aber, J. L. (2011). Two-year impacts of a universal school-based social-emotional and literacy intervention: An experiment in translational developmental research. *Child Development*, 82(2), 533–554. https://doi.org/10.1111/j.1467-8624.2010.01560.x.

Kampis, D., & Southgate, V. (2020). Altercentric cognition: How others influence our cognitive processing. *Trends in Cognitive Sciences*, 24(11), 945–959. https://doi.org/10.1016/j.tics.2020.09.003.

Kavanaugh, R. D. (2006). Pretend play and Theory of Mind. In L. Balter & C. S. Tamis-LeMonda, eds., *Child psychology: A handbook of contemporary issues*. Psychology Press, pp. 153–166.

Kellman, P. J., & Spelke, E. S. (1983). Perception of partly occluded objects in infancy. *Cognitive Psychology*, 15(4), 483–524. https://doi.org/10.1016/0010-0285(83)90017-8.

Kloo, D., Kristen-Antonow, S., & Sodian, B. (2020). Progressing from an implicit to an explicit false belief understanding: A matter of executive control? *International Journal of Behavioral Development*, 44(2), 107–115. https://doi.org/10.1177/0165025419850901.

Kloo, D., & Perner, J. (2003). Training transfer between card sorting and false belief understanding: Helping children apply conflicting descriptions. *Child Development*, 74(6), 1823–1839. https://doi.org/10.1046/j.1467-8624.2003.00640.x.

Knudsen, B., & Liszkowski, U. (2011). 18-month-olds predict specific action mistakes through attribution of false belief, not ignorance, and intervene accordingly. *Infancy*, 17(6), 672–691. https://doi.org/10.1111/j.1467-7687.2011.01098.x.

Kominsky, J. F. (2022). The challenges of improving infant research methods. *Infant and Child Development*, 31(5), e2332. https://doi.org/10.1002/icd.2332.

Kovács, Á. M., Téglás, E., & Endress, A. D. (2010). The social sense: Susceptibility to others' beliefs in human infants and adults. *Science*, 330(6012), 1830–1834. https://doi.org/10.1126/science.1190792.

Krupenye C., & Call, J. (2019). Theory of Mind in animals: Current and future directions. *WIREs Cogn Sci*, 10, e1503. https://doi.org/10.1002/wcs.1503.

Kulke, L., & Rakoczy, H. (2018). Implicit Theory of Mind – an overview of current replications and non-replications. *Data in Brief*, 16, 101–104. https://doi.org/10.1016/j.dib.2017.11.016.

Lane, J. D., & Bowman, L. C. (2021). How children's social tendencies can shape their Theory of Mind development: Access and attention to social information. *Developmental Review*, 61, 100977. https://doi.org/10.1016/j.dr.2021.100977.

Lecce, S., Bianco, F., Devine, R. T., & Hughes, C. (2017). Relations between Theory of Mind and executive function in middle childhood: A short-term longitudinal study. *Journal of Experimental Child Psychology*, 163, 69–86. https://doi.org/10.1016/j.jecp.2017.06.011.

Lecce, S., Bianco, F., Devine, R. T., Hughes, C., & Banerjee, R. (2014). Promoting Theory of Mind during middle childhood: A training program. *Journal of Experimental Child Psychology*, 126, 52–67. https://doi.org/10.1016/j.jecp.2014.03.002.

Lecce, S., Caputi, M., & Hughes, C. (2011). Does sensitivity to criticism mediate the relationship between theory of mind and academic achievement? *Journal of Experimental Child Psychology*, 110(3), 313–331. https://doi.org/10.1016/j.jecp.2011.04.011.

Lecce, S., & Devine, R. T. (2021). Social interaction in early and middle childhood: The role of theory of mind. In H. Ferguson & E. Bradford, eds., *The cognitive basis of social interaction across the lifespan*. Oxford University Press, pp. 46–68. https://doi.org/10.1093/oso/9780198843290.003.0003.

Lee, J. Y. S., & Imuta, K. (2021). Lying and Theory of Mind: A meta-analysis. *Child Development*, 92, 536–553. https://doi.org/10.1111/cdev.13535.

Leslie, A. M. (1987). Pretense and representation: The origins of "Theory of Mind." *Psychological Review*, 94(4), 412–426. https://doi.org/10.1037/0033-295X.94.4.412.

Leslie, A. M. (1994). Pretending and believing: Issues in the theory of ToMM. *Cognition*, 50(1-3), 211–238. https://doi.org/10.1016/0010-0277(94)90029-9.

Lewis, C., Huang, Z., & Rooksby, M. (2006). Chinese preschoolers' false belief understanding: Is social knowledge underpinned by parental styles, social interactions or executive functions? *Psychologia*, 49(4), 252–266. https://doi.org/10.2117/psysoc.2006.252.

Licata, M., Paulus, M., Thoermer, C. et al. (2014). Mother–infant interaction quality and infants' ability to encode actions as goal-directed. *Social Development*, 23(2), 340–356. https://doi.org/10.1111/sode.12057.

Liu, D., Wellman, H. M., Tardif, T., & Sabbagh, M. A. (2008). Theory of Mind development in Chinese children: A meta-analysis of false-belief understanding across cultures and languages. *Developmental Psychology*, 44(2), 523–531. https://doi.org/10.1037/0012-1649.44.2.523.

Liu, Y., Moss, E., Ting, F., & Hyde, D. C. (2025). Neural sensitivity to others' belief states in infancy predicts later theory of mind reasoning in childhood. *Cortex*, 184, 96–105. https://doi.org/10.1016/j.cortex.2024.11.023.

Lohmann, H., & Tomasello, M. (2003). The role of language in the development of false belief understanding: A training study. *Child Development*, 74(4), 1130–1144. https://doi.org/10.1111/1467-8624.00597.

Low, J. (2010). Preschoolers' implicit and explicit false-belief understanding: Relations with complex syntactical mastery. *Child Development*, 81(2), 597–615. https://doi.org/10.1111/j.1467-8624.2009.01418.x.

Low, J., Apperly, I. A., Butterfill, S. A., & Rakoczy, H. (2016). Cognitive architecture of belief reasoning in children and adults: A Primer on the two-systems account. *Child Development Perspectives*, 10(3), 184–189. https://doi.org/10.1111/cdep.12183.

Low, J., & Watts, J. (2013). Attributing false beliefs about object identity reveals a signature blind spot in humans' efficient mind-reading system. *Psychological Science*, 24(3), 305–311. https://doi.org/10.1177/0956797612451469.

Mahy, C. E., Moses, L. J., & Pfeifer, J. H. (2014). How and where: theory-of-mind in the brain. *Dev Cogn Neurosci.*, 9, 68–81. https://doi.org/10.1016/j.dcn.2014.01.002.

Main, M. (1991). Metacognitive knowledge, metacognitive monitoring, and singular (coherent) vs. multiple (incoherent) model of attachment: Findings and directions for future research. In C. M. Parkes, J. Stevenson-Hinde, & P. Marris, eds., *Attachment across the life cycle*. Tavistock/Routledge, pp. 127–159.

Manzi, F., Peretti, G., Di Dio, C. et al. (2020). A robot is not worth another: Exploring children's mental state attribution to different humanoid robots. *Frontiers in Psychology*, 11, 2011. https://doi.org/10.3389/fpsyg.2020.02011.

Marchetti, A., Manzi, F., Itakura, S., & Massaro, D. (2018). Theory of Mind and humanoid robots from a lifespan perspective. *Zeitschrift für Psychologie*, 226(2), 98–109. https://doi.org/10.1027/2151-2604/a000326.

Marcovitch, S., O'Brien, M., Calkins, S. D. et al. (2015). A longitudinal assessment of the relation between executive function and Theory of Mind at 3, 4, and 5 Years. *Cognitive Development*, 33, 40–55. https://doi.org/10.1016/j.cogdev.2014.07.001.

Masten, A. S., & Cicchetti, D. (2010). Developmental cascades [Editorial]. *Development and Psychopathology*, 22(3), 491–495. https://doi.org/10.1017/S0954579410000222.

Mayer, A., & Träuble, B. E. (2013). Synchrony in the onset of mental state understanding across cultures? A study among children in Samoa. *International Journal of Behavioral Development*, 37(1), 21–28. https://doi.org/10.1177/0165025412454030.

McAlister, A., & Peterson, C. (2007). A longitudinal study of child siblings and Theory of Mind development. *Cognitive Development*, 22(2), 258–270. https://doi.org/10.1016/j.cogdev.2006.10.009.

McMahon, C. A., & Bernier, A. (2017). Twenty years of research on parental mind-mindedness: Empirical findings, theoretical and methodological challenges, and new directions. *Developmental Review*, 46, 54–80. https://doi.org/10.1016/j.dr.2017.07.001.

Meins, E. (2012). Social relationships and children's understanding of mind. In M. Siegal & L. Surian, eds., *Access to language and cognitive development*. Oxford University Press, pp. 1134–1145.

Meins, E., Fernyhough, C., Arnott, B., Leekam, S. R., & de Rosnay, M. (2013). Mind-mindedness and Theory of Mind: Mediating roles of language and perspectival symbolic play. *Child Development*, 84(5), 1777–1790. https://doi.org/10.1111/cdev.12061.

Meins, E., Fernyhough, C., de Rosnay, M. et al. (2012). Mind-mindedness as a multidimensional construct: Appropriate and nonattuned mind-related comments independently predict infant–mother attachment in a socially diverse sample. *Infancy*, 17(4), 393–415. https://doi.org/10.1111/j.1532-7078.2011.00087.x.

Meins, E., Fernyhough, C., Russell, J., & Clark-Carter, D. (1998). Security of attachment as a predictor of symbolic and mentalising abilities: A longitudinal study. *Social Development*, 7(1), 1–24. https://doi.org/10.1111/1467-9507.00047.

Meins, E., Fernyhough, C., Wainwright, R. et al. (2003). Pathways to understanding mind: Construct validity and predictive validity of maternal mind-mindedness. *Child Development*, 74(4), 1194–1211. https://doi.org/10.1111/1467-8624.00601.

Meins, E., Fernyhough, C., Wainwright, R. et al. (2002). Maternal mind-Mindedness and attachment security as predictors of Theory of Mind understanding. *Child Development*, 73(6), 1715–1726. https://doi.org/10.1111/1467-8624.00501.

Meltzoff, A. N. (1995). Understanding the intentions of others: Re-enactment of intended acts by 18-month-old children. *Developmental Psychology*, 31(5), 838–850. https://doi.org/10.1037/0012-1649.31.5.838.

Meltzoff, A. N., Gopnik, A., & Repacholi, B. M. (1999). Toddlers' understanding of intentions, desires, and emotions: Explorations of the dark ages. In P. D. Zelazo, J. W. Astington, & D. R. Olson, eds., *Developing theories of intention*. Taylor & Francis Group, pp. 17–42.

Miller, S. A. (2009). Children's understanding of second-order mental states. *Psychological Bulletin*, 135(5), 749–773. https://doi.org/10.1037/a0016854.

Miller, S. A. (2012). *Theory of Mind: Beyond the preschool years*. Psychology Press.

Miller, S. A. (2016). *Parenting and Theory of Mind*. Oxford University Press.

Milligan, K., Astington, J. W., & Dack, L. A. (2007). Language and Theory of Mind: Meta-analysis of the relation between language ability and false-belief understanding. *Child Development*, 78(2), 622–646. https://doi.org/10.1111/j.1467-8624.2007.01018.x.

Miyake, A., Friedman, N. P., Emerson, M. J. et al. (2000). The unity and diversity of executive functions and their contributions to complex "frontal lobe" tasks: A latent variable analysis. *Cognitive Psychology*, 41(1), 49–100. https://doi.org/10.1016/j.cortex.2016.04.023.

Moll, H., Khalulyan, A., & Moffett, L. (2016). 2.5-year-Olds Express suspense when others approach reality with false expectations. *Child Development*, 88(1), 114–122. https://doi.org/10.1111/cdev.12581.

Moriguchi, Y., & Shinohara, I. (2019). Socioeconomic disparity in prefrontal development during early childhood. *Scientific Reports*, 9(1), 2585. https://doi.org/10.1038/s41598-019-39255-6.

Moses, L. J. (2001). Executive accounts of theory-of-mind development. *Child Development*, 72(3), 688–690. https://doi.org/10.1111/1467-8624.00306.

Moses, L. J., & Tahiroglu, D. (2010). Clarifying the relation between executive function and children's theories of mind. *Self- and Social-Regulation*, 218–233. https://doi.org/10.1093/acprof:oso/9780195327694.003.0009.

Murray, L., Woolgar, M., Briers, S., & Hipwell, A. (1999). Children's social representations in dolls' house and Theory of Mind tasks, and their relation to family adversity and child disturbance. *Social Development*, 8(2), 179–200. https://doi.org/10.1111/1467-9507.00090.

Nelson, P. B., Adamson, L. B., & Bakeman, R. (2008). Toddlers' joint engagement experience facilitates preschoolers' acquisition of Theory of Mind.

Developmental Science, 11(6), 847–852. https://doi.org/10.1111/j.1467-7687.2008.00733.x.

Nguyen, T.-K., & Astington, J. W. (2014). Reassessing the bilingual advantage in Theory of Mind and its cognitive underpinnings. *Bilingualism: Language and Cognition*, 17(2), 396–409. https://doi.org/10.1017/S1366728913000394.

Olineck, K. M., & Poulin-Dubois, D. (2007). Imitation of intentional actions and internal state language in infancy predict preschool Theory of Mind skills. *European Journal of Developmental Psychology*, 4(1), 14–30. https://doi.org/10.1080/17405620601046931.

Olson, S. L., Lopez-Duran, N., Lunkenheimer, E. S., Chang, H., & Sameroff, A. J. (2011). Individual differences in the development of early peer aggression: Integrating contributions of self-regulation, Theory of Mind, and parenting. *Development and Psychopathology*, 23(1), 253–266. https://doi.org/10.1017/S0954579410000775.

Onishi, K. H., & Baillargeon, R. (2005). Do 15-month-old infants understand false beliefs? *Science*, 308(5719), 255–258. https://doi.org/10.1126/science.1107621.

O'Reilly, J., & Peterson, C. C. (2014). Theory of Mind at home: Linking authoritative and authoritarian parenting styles to children's social understanding. *Early Child Development and Care*, 184(12), 1934–1947. https://doi.org/10.1080/03004430.2014.894034.

Ornaghi, V., Brockmeier, J., & Gavazzi, I. G. (2011). The role of language games in children's understanding of mental states: A training study. *Journal of Cognition and Development*, 12(2), 239–259. https://doi.org/10.1080/15248372.2011.563487.

Ornaghi, V., Brockmeier, J., & Grazzani, I. (2014). Enhancing social cognition by training children in emotion understanding: A primary school study. *Journal of Experimental Child Psychology*, 119, 26–39. https://doi.org/10.1016/j.jecp.2013.10.005.

Osterhaus, C., & Bosacki, S. L. (2022). Looking for the lighthouse: A systematic review of advanced theory-of-mind tests beyond preschool. *Developmental Review*, 64, 1–23. https://doi.org/10.1016/j.dr.2022.101021.

Ozonoff, S., & McEvoy, R. E. (2008). A longitudinal study of executive function and Theory of Mind development in autism. *Development and Psychopathology*, 6(3), 415–431. https://doi.org/10.1017/S0954579400006027.

Paulus, M. (2022). Should infant psychology rely on the violation-of-expectation method? Not anymore. *Infant and Child Development*, 31(1), e2306. https://doi.org/10.1002/icd.2306.

Pavarini, G., de Hollanda Souza, D., & Hawk, C. K. (2013). Parental practices and Theory of Mind development. *Child and Family Studies*, 22(6), 844–853. https://doi.org/10.1007/s10826-012-9643-8.

Pears, K. C., & Moses, L. J. (2003). Demographics, parenting, and Theory of Mind in preschool children. *Social Development*, 12(1), 1–19. https://doi.org/10.1111/1467-9507.00219.

Pellicano, E. (2007). Links between Theory of Mind and executive function in young children with autism: Clues to developmental primacy. *Developmental Psychology*, 43(4), 974–990. https://doi.org/10.1037/0012-1649.43.4.974.

Perner, J. (1991). *Understanding the representational mind*. The MIT Press.

Perner, J. (2010). Who took the cog out of cognitive science? Mentalism in an era of anti-cognitivism. In P. A. Frensch & R. Schwarzer, eds., *Cognition and neuropsychology: International perspectives on psychological science*. Psychology Press, pp. 241–261.

Perner, J., & Lang, B. (1999). Development of Theory of Mind and executive control. *Trends in Cognitive Sciences*, 3(9), 337–344. https://doi.org/10.1016/S1364-6613(99)01362-5.

Perner, J., Lang, B., & Kloo, D. (2002). Theory of Mind and self-control: More than a common problem of inhibition. *Child Development*, 73(3), 752–767. https://doi.org/10.1111/1467-8624.00436.

Perner, J., & Ruffman, T. (2005). Infants' insight into the mind: How deep? *Science*, 308(5719), 214–216. https://doi.org/10.1126/science.1111656.

Perner, J., Ruffman, T., & Leekam, S. R. (1994). Theory of Mind is contagious: You catch it from your sibs. *Child Development*, 65(4), 1228–1238. https://doi.org/10.2307/1131316.

Peterson, C. C. (2000). Kindred spirits. *Cognitive Development*, 15(4), 435–455. https://doi.org/10.1016/S0885-2014(01)00040-5.

Peterson, C., & Slaughter, V. (2003). Opening windows into the mind: Mothers' preferences for mental state explanations and children's Theory of Mind. *Cognitive Development*, 18(3), 399–429. https://doi.org/10.1016/S0885-2014(03)00041-8.

Peterson, C. C., & Slaughter, V. (2017). Culture and the sequence of developmental milestones toward Theory of Mind mastery. In V. Slaughter & M. de Rosnay, eds., *Theory of Mind development in context*. Routledge/Taylor & Francis Group, pp. 25–40. https://doi.org/10.1037/a0023899.

Peterson, B. K., Weber, J. N., Kay, E. H., Fisher, H. S., & Hoekstra, H. E. (2012). Double digest RADseq: An inexpensive method for de novo SNP discovery and genotyping in model and non-model species. *PLOS ONE*, 7(5), e37135. https://doi.org/10.1371/journal.pone.0037135.

Peterson, C. C., & Wellman, H. M. (2009). From fancy to reason: Scaling deaf and hearing children's understanding of Theory of Mind and pretence. *British Journal of Developmental Psychology*, 27(2), 297–310. https://doi.org/10.1348/026151008X299728.

Peterson, C. C., Wellman, H. M., & Slaughter, V. (2012). The mind behind the message: Advancing theory-of-mind scales for typically developing children, and those with deafness, autism, or Asperger syndrome. *Child Development*, 83(2), 469–485. https://doi.org/10.1111/j.1467-8624.2011.01728.x.

Peterson, C., Park, N., & Seligman, M. E. (2005). Orientations to happiness and life satisfaction: The full life versus the empty life. *Happiness Studies*, 6(1), 25–41. https://doi.org/10.1007/s10902-004-1278-z.

Piaget, J., & Inhelder, B. (1967). *The child's conception of space*. W. W. Norton.

Poulin-Dubois, D. (1999). Les précurseurs d'une théorie de l'esprit dans la première enfance: Mythes et réalités. *Enfance*, 52(3), 322–326.

Poulin-Dubois, D., Azar, N., Elkaim, B., & Burnside, K. (2020). Testing the stability of Theory of Mind: A longitudinal approach. *PLOS ONE*, 15(11), e0241721. https://doi.org/10.1371/journal.pone.0241721.

Poulin-Dubois, D., Dutemple, E., & Burnside, K. (2021). Naïve theories of biology, physics, and psychology in children with ASD. *Autism and Developmental Disorders*, 51(10), 3600–3609. https://doi.org/10.1007/s10803-020-04813-9.

Poulin-Dubois, D., Frank, I., Graham, S., & Elkin, A. (1999). The role of shape similarity in toddlers' lexical extensions. *British Journal of Developmental Psychology*, 17(Part 1), 21–36. https://doi.org/10.1348/026151099165131.

Poulin-Dubois, D., & Goldman, E. J. (2023). Is false belief understanding stable from infancy to childhood? We don't know yet. *Cognitive Development*, 66, 101309. https://doi.org/10.1016/j.cogdev.2023.101309.

Poulin-Dubois, D., Goldman, E. J., Meltzer, A., & Psaradellis, E. (2023). Discontinuity from implicit to explicit Theory of Mind from infancy to preschool age. *Cognitive Development*, 65, 101273. https://doi.org/10.1016/j.cogdev.2022.101273.

Poulin-Dubois, D., Hastings, P. D., Chiarella, S. S. et al. (2018). The eyes know it: Toddlers' visual scanning of sad faces is predicted by their Theory of Mind skills. *PLOS ONE*, 13(12), e0208524. https://doi.org/10.1371/journal.pone.0208524.

Poulin-Dubois, D. & Tilden, J. (1996, April). *Infants' understanding of desires*. Poster presented at the 10th Biennial International Conference on Infant Studies, Providence, RI.

Poulin-Dubois, D., & Yott, J. (2014). Fonctions exécutives et théorie de l'esprit chez le Jeune Enfant: Une Relation réciproque? *Psychologie Française*, 59(1), 59–69. http://dx.doi.org/10.1016/j.psfr.2013.11.002.

Premack, D., & Woodruff, G. (1978). Does the chimpanzee have a Theory of Mind? *Behavioral and Brain Sciences*, 1(4), 515–526. https://doi.org/10.1017/S0140525X00076512.

Quesque, F., & Rossetti, Y. (2020). What do theory-of-mind tasks actually measure? Theory and practice. *Perspectives on Psychological Science*, 15(2), 384–396. https://doi.org/10.1177/1745691619896607.

Remmel, E., & Peters, K. (2008). Theory of Mind and language in children with cochlear implants. *Deaf Studies and Deaf Education*, 14(2), 218–236. https://doi.org/10.1093/deafed/enn036.

Repacholi, B. M., & Gopnik, A. (1997). Early reasoning about desires: Evidence from 14- and 18-month-olds. *Developmental Psychology*, 33(1), 12–21. https://doi.org/10.1037/0012-1649.33.1.12.

Repacholi, B. M., & Slaughter, V. (2003). *Individual differences in Theory of Mind: Implications for typical and atypical development*. Psychology Press. https://doi.org/10.4324/9780203488508.

Richardson, H., Lisandrelli, G., Riobueno-Naylor, A., & Saxe, R. (2018). Development of the social brain from age three to twelve years. *Nature Communications*, 9(1), 1027. https://doi.org/10.1038/s41467-018-03399-2.

Ruffman, T. (2014). To belief or not belief: Children's Theory of Mind. *Developmental Review*, 34(3), 265–293. https://doi.org/10.1016/j.dr.2014.04.001.

Ruffman, T. (2023). Belief it or not: How children construct a Theory of Mind. *Child Development Perspectives*, 17, 106–112. https://doi.org/10.1111/cdep.12483.

Ruffman, T., Aitken, J., Wilson, A., Puri, A., & Taumoepeau, M. (2018). A re-examination of the Broccoli Task: Implications for children's understanding of subjective desire. *Cognitive Development*, 46, 79–85. https://doi.org/10.1016/j.cogdev.2017.08.001.

Ruffman, T., Chen, L., Lorimer, B. et al. (2023). Exposure to behavioral regularities in everyday life predicts infants' acquisition of Mental State Vocabulary. *Developmental Science*, 26(4), e13343. https://doi.org/10.1111/desc.13343.

Ruffman, T., Perner, J., & Parkin, L. (1999). How parenting style affects false belief understanding. *Social Development*, 8(3), 395–411. https://doi.org/10.1111/1467-9507.00103.

Ruffman, T., Perner, J., Naito, M., Parkin, L., & Clements, W. A. (1998). Older (but not younger) siblings facilitate false belief understanding. *Developmental Psychology*, 34(1), 161–174. https://doi.org/10.1037/0012-1649.34.1.161.

Ruffman, T., Slade, L., & Crowe, E. (2002). The relation between children's and Mothers' Mental State Language and theory-of-mind understanding. *Child Development*, 73(3), 734–751. https://doi.org/10.1111/1467-8624.00435.

Ruffman, T., Slade, L., Devitt, K., & Crowe, E. (2006). What mothers say and what they do: The relation between parenting, Theory of Mind, language and conflict/cooperation. *British Journal of Developmental Psychology*, 24(1), 105–124. https://doi.org/10.1348/026151005X82848.

Ruffman, T., Slade, L., Rowlandson, K., Rumsey, C., & Garnham, A. (2003). How language relates to belief, desire, and emotion understanding. *Cognitive Development*, 18(2), 139–158. https://doi.org/10.1016/S0885-2014(03)00002-9.

Russell, J. (1996). *Agency: Its role in mental development*. Erlbaum (UK) Taylor & Francis. https://doi.org/10.4324/9780203775691.

Russell, J., Mauthner, N., Sharpe, S., & Tidswell, T. (1991). The "windows task" as a measure of strategic deception in preschoolers and autistic subjects. *British Journal of Developmental Psychology*, 9(2), 331–349. https://doi.org/10.1111/j.2044-835X.1991.tb00881.x.

Sabbagh, M. A., Bowman, L. C., Evraire, L. E., & Ito, J. M. (2009). Neurodevelopmental correlates of Theory of Mind in preschool children. *Child Development*, 80(4), 1147–1162. https://doi.org/10.1111/j.1467-8624.2009.01322.x.

Sabbagh, M. A., & Paulus, M. (2018). Replication studies of implicit false belief with infants and toddlers. *Cognitive Development*, 46, 1–3. https://doi.org/10.1016/j.cogdev.2018.07.003.

Sabbagh, M. A., Xu, F., Carlson, S. M., Moses, L. J., & Lee, K. (2006). The development of executive functioning and Theory of Mind. *Psychological Science*, 17(1), 74–81. https://doi.org/10.1111/j.1467-9280.2005.01667.x.

Sai, L., Shang, S., Tay, C. et al. (2021) Theory of Mind, executive function, and lying in children: A meta-analysis. *Developmental Science*, 24, e13096. https://doi.org/10.1111/desc.13096.

Samson, D., Apperly, I. A., Braithwaite, J. J., Andrews, B. J., & Bodley Scott, S. E. (2010). Seeing it their way: Evidence for rapid and involuntary computation of what other people see. *Psychology: Human Perception and Performance*, 36(5), 1255–1266. https://doi.org/10.1037/a0018729.

Saxe, R. R., Whitfield-Gabrieli, S., Scholz, J., & Pelphrey, K. A. (2009). Brain regions for perceiving and reasoning about other people in school-aged children. *Child Development*, 80(4), 1197–1209. https://doi.org/10.1111/j.1467-8624.2009.01325.x.

Schneider, D., Lam, R., Bayliss, A. P., & Dux, P. E. (2012). Cognitive load disrupts implicit theory-of-mind processing. *Psychological Science*, 23(8), 842–847. https://doi.org/10.1177/0956797612439070.

Schneider, W., Lockl, K., & Fernandez, O. (2005). Interrelationships among Theory of Mind, executive control, language development, and working memory in young children: a Longitudinal analysis. In W. Schneider, R. Schumann-Hengsteler, & B. Sodian, eds., *Young children's cognitive development: Interrelationships among executive functioning, working memory, verbal ability, and Theory of Mind*. Lawrence Erlbaum Associates, pp. 259–284.

Scholl, B. J., & Leslie, A. M. (1999). Modularity, development and 'theory of mind.' *Mind & Language*, 14(1), 131–153. https://doi.org/10.1111/1468-0017.00106.

Scholl, B. J., & Tremoulet, P. D. (2000). Perceptual causality and animacy. *Trends in Cognitive Sciences*, 4(8), 299–309. https://doi.org/10.1016/S1364-6613(00)01506-0.

Schroeder, S. R. (2018). Do bilinguals have an advantage in Theory of Mind? A meta-analysis. *Frontiers in Communication*, 3(9). https://doi.org/10.3389/fcomm.2018.00036.

Schurz, M., Radua, J., Aichhorn, M., Richlan, F., & Perner, J. (2014). Fractionating theory of mind: A meta-analysis of functional brain imaging studies. *Neuroscience & Biobehavioral Reviews*, 42, 9–34. https://doi.org/10.1016/j.neubiorev.2014.01.009.

Schuwerk, T., Jarvers, I., Vuori, M., & Sodian, B. (2016). Implicit mentalizing persists beyond early childhood and is profoundly impaired in children with autism spectrum condition. *Frontiers in Psychology*, 7(1696). https://doi.org/10.3389/fpsyg.2016.01696.

Schuwerk, T., Kampis, D., Baillargeon, R. et al. (2025). (accepted pending data collection). Action anticipation based on an agent's epistemic state in toddlers and adults. *Child Development*.

Scott, R. M. (2017). Surprise! 20-month-old infants understand the emotional consequences of false beliefs. *Cognition*, 159, 33–47. https://doi.org/10.1016/j.cognition.2016.11.005.

Scott, R. M., & Baillargeon, R. (2017). Early false-belief understanding. *Trends in Cognitive Sciences*, 21(4), 237–249. https://doi.org/10.1016/j.tics.2017.01.012.

Selcuk, B., Gonultas, S., & Ekerim-Akbulut, M. (2023). Development and use of Theory of Mind in social and cultural context. *Child Development Perspectives*, 17(1), 39–45. https://doi.org/10.1111/cdep.12473.

References

Selman, R. L. (1971). Taking another's perspective: Role-taking development in early childhood. *Child Development*, 42(6), 1721–1734. https://doi.org/10.2307/1127580.

Senju, A. (2012). Spontaneous Theory of Mind and its absence in autism spectrum disorders. *The Neuroscientist*, 18(2), 108–113. https://doi.org/10.1177/1073858410397208.

Setoh, P., Scott, R. M., & Baillargeon, R. (2016). Two-and-a-half-year-olds succeed at a traditional false-belief task with reduced processing demands. *Proceedings of the National Academy of Sciences*, 113(47), 13360–13365. https://doi.org/10.1073/pnas.1609203113.

Shahaeian, A., Nielsen, M., Peterson, C. C., & Slaughter, V. (2014). Iranian mothers' disciplinary strategies and Theory of Mind in children. *Cross-Cultural Psychology*, 45(7), 1110–1123. https://doi.org/10.1177/0022022114534772.

Shahaeian, A., Peterson, C. C., Slaughter, V., & Wellman, H. M. (2011). Culture and the sequence of steps in Theory of Mind development. *Developmental Psychology*, 47(5), 1239–1247. https://doi.org/10.1037/a0023899.

Sharp, C., & Fonagy, P. (2008). The parent's capacity to treat the child as a psychological agent: Constructs, measures and implications for developmental psychopathology. *Social Development*, 17(3), 737–754. https://doi.org/10.1111/j.1467-9507.2007.00457.x.

Slade, L., & Ruffman, T. (2005). How language does (and does not) relate to Theory of Mind: A longitudinal study of syntax, semantics, working memory and false belief. *British Journal of Developmental Psychology*, 23(1), 117–141. https://doi.org/10.1348/026151004X21332.

Slaughter, V., Dennis, M. J., & Pritchard, M. (2002). Theory of mind and peer acceptance in preschool children. *British Journal of Developmental Psychology*, 20(4), 545–564. https://doi.org/10.1348/026151002760390945.

Slaughter, V., & Perez-Zapata, D. (2014). Cultural variations in the development of mind reading. *Child Development Perspectives*, 8(4), 237–241. https://doi.org/10.1111/cdep.12091.

Slaughter, V., Imuta, K., Peterson, C. C., & Henry, J. D. (2015). Meta-analysis of Theory of Mind and peer popularity in the preschool and early school years. *Child Development*, 86(4), 1159–1174. https://doi.org/10.1111/cdev.12372.

Sodian, B., Kaltefleiter, L. J., Schuwerk, T., & Kloo, D. (2024). Continuity in false belief understanding from 33 to 52 months of age. *Journal of Experimental Child Psychology*, 247, 106039. https://doi.org/10.1016/j.jecp.2024.106039.

Sodian, B., Licata, M., Kristen-Antonow, S. et al. (2016). Understanding of goals, beliefs, and desires predicts morally relevant Theory of Mind: A longitudinal investigation. *Child Development*, 87(4), 1221–1232. https://doi.org/10.1111/cdev.12533.

Sodian, B., & Kristen-Antonow, S. (2015). Declarative joint attention as a foundation of Theory of Mind. *Developmental Psychology*, 51(9), 1190–1200. https://doi.org/10.1037/dev0000039.

Sodian, B., Kristen-Antonow, S., & Kloo, D. (2020). How does children's Theory of Mind become explicit? A review of longitudinal findings. *Child Development Perspectives*, 14(3), 171–177. https://doi.org/10.1111/cdep.12381.

Sodian, B., Thoermer, C., & Metz, U. (2007). Now I see it but you don't: 14-month-olds can represent another person's visual perspective. *Developmental Science*, 10(2), 199–204. https://doi.org/10.1111/j.1467-7687.2007.00580.x.

Southgate, V. (2020). Are infants altercentric? The other and the self in early social cognition. *Psychological Review*, 127(4), 505–523. https://doi.org/10.1037/rev0000182.

Southgate, V., Senju, A., & Csibra, G. (2007). Action anticipation through attribution of false belief by 2-year-olds. *Psychological Science*, 18(7), 587–592. https://doi.org/10.1111/j.1467-9280.2007.01944.x.

Southgate, V., Chevallier, C., & Csibra, G. (2010). Seventeen-month-olds appeal to false beliefs to interpret others' referential communication. *Developmental Science*, 13(6), 907–912. https://doi.org/10.1111/j.1467-7687.2009.00946.x.

Spelke, E. S. (2022). *What babies know: Core knowledge and composition.* Oxford University Press.

Sroufe, L. A., Egeland, B., Carlson, E., & Collins, W. A. (2005). Placing early attachment experiences in developmental context: The Minnesota longitudinal study. In K. E. Grossmann, K. Grossmann, & E. Waters, eds., *Attachment from infancy to adulthood: The major longitudinal studies.* New York: Guilford, pp. 48–70.

Steele, H., Steele, M., & Fonagy, P. (1996). Associations among attachment classifications of mothers, fathers, and their infants: Evidence for a relationship-specific perspective. *Child Development*, 67, 541–555. https://doi.org/10.2307/1131831.

Stower, R., Calvo-Barajas, N., Castellano, G., & Kappas, A. (2021). A meta-analysis on children's trust in Social Robots. *International Journal of Social Robotics*, 13(8), 1979–2001. https://doi.org/10.1007/s12369-020-00736-8.

Surian, L., & Caldi, S. (2010). Infants' individuation of agents and inert objects. *Developmental Science*, 13(1), 143–150. https://doi.org/10.1111/j.1467-7687.2009.00873.x.

Surian, L., & Franchin, L. (2020). On the domain specificity of the mechanisms underpinning spontaneous anticipatory looks in false-belief tasks. *Developmental Science*, 23(6), e12955. https://doi.org/10.1111/desc.12955.

Surian, L., & Geraci, A. (2012). Where will the triangle look for it? attributing false beliefs to a geometric shape at 17 months. *British Journal of Developmental Psychology*, 30(1), 30–44. https://doi.org/10.1111/j.2044-835X.2011.02046.x.

Szpak, M., & Białecka-Pikul, M. (2020). Links between attachment and Theory of Mind in childhood: Meta-analytic review. *Social Development*, 29(3), 653–673. https://doi.org/10.1111/sode.12432.

Tahiroglu, D., Moses, L. J., Carlson, S. M. et al. (2014). The children's social understanding scale: Construction and validation of a parent-report measure for assessing individual differences in children's theories of mind. *Developmental Psychology*, 50(11), 2485–2497. https://doi.org/10.1037/a0037914.

Tardif, T., & Wellman, H. M. (2000). Acquisition of mental state language in Mandarin- and Cantonese-speaking children. *Developmental Psychology*, 36(1), 25–43. https://doi.org/10.1037/0012-1649.36.1.25.

Tare, M., & Gelman, S. A. (2010). Determining that a label is kind-referring: Factors that influence children's and adults' novel word extensions. *Child Language*, 37(5), 1007–1026. https://doi.org/10.1017/S0305000909990134.

Thoermer, C., Sodian, B., Vuori, M., Perst, H., & Kristen, S. (2011). Continuity from an implicit to an explicit understanding of false belief from infancy to preschool age. *British Journal of Developmental Psychology*, 30(1), 172–187. https://doi.org/10.1111/j.2044-835X.2011.02067.x.

Tomasello, M. (2018). How children come to understand false beliefs: A shared intentionality account. *PNAS Proceedings of the National Academy of Sciences of the United States of America*, 115(34), 8491–8498. https://doi.org/10.1073/pnas.1804761115.

Tompkins, V. (2015). Improving low-income preschoolers' Theory of Mind: A training study. *Cognitive Development*, 36, 1–19. https://doi.org/10.1016/j.cogdev.2015.07.001.

Tompkins, V., Benigno, J. P., Kiger Lee, B., & Wright, B. M. (2018). The relation between parents' mental state talk and children's Social Understanding:

A meta-analysis. *Social Development*, 27(2), 223–246. https://doi.org/10.1111/sode.12280.

Turk-Browne, N. B., & Aslin, R. N. (2024). Infant neuroscience: How to measure brain activity in the youngest minds. *Trends in Neurosciences*, 47(5), 338–354. https://doi.org/10.1016/j.tins.2024.02.003.

van IJzendoorn, M. H., Dijkstra, J., & Bus, A. G. (1995). Attachment, intelligence, and language: A meta-analysis. *Social Development*, 4(2), 115–128. https://doi.org/10.1111/j.1467-9507.1995.tb00055.x.

Vinden, P. G. (2001). Parenting attitudes and children's understanding of mind: A comparison of Korean American and Anglo-American families. *Cognitive Development*, 16(3), 793–809. https://doi.org/10.1016/S0885-2014(01)00059-4.

Wade, M., Prime, H., Jenkins, J. M. et al. (2018). On the relation between Theory of Mind and executive functioning: A developmental cognitive neuroscience perspective. *Psychon Bull Rev*, 25(6), 2119–2140. https://doi.org/10.3758/s13423-018-1459-0.

Watson, A. C., Nixon, C. L., Wilson, A., & Capage, L. (1999). Social interaction skills and theory of mind in young children. *Developmental Psychology*, 35(2), 386–391. https://doi.org/10.1037/0012-1649.35.2.386.

Watson, A. C., Painter, K. M., & Bornstein, M. H. (2001). Longitudinal relations between 2-year-olds' language and 4-year-olds' theory of mind. *Journal of Cognition and Development*, 2(4), 449–445. https://doi.org/10.1207/S15327647JCD0204_5.

Wellman, H. M. (1990). *The child's Theory of Mind*. MIT Press.

Wellman, II. M. (2014). *Making minds: How Theory of Mind develops*. Oxford University Press.

Wellman, H. M. (2017). The development of Theory of Mind: Historical reflections. *Child Development Perspectives*, 11(3), 207–214. https://doi.org/10.1111/cdep.12236.

Wellman, H. M., & Banerjee, M. (1991). Mind and emotion: Children's understanding of the emotional consequences of beliefs and desires. *British Journal of Developmental Psychology*, 9, 191–214. https://doi.org/10.1111/j.2044-835X.1991.tb00871.x.

Wellman, H. M., Cross, D., & Watson, J. (2001). Meta-analysis of theory-of-mind development: The truth about false belief. *Child Development*, 72(3), 655–684. https://doi.org/10.1111/1467-8624.00304.

Wellman, H. M., & Liu, D. (2004). Scaling of theory-of-mind tasks. *Child Development*, 75(2), 523–541. https://doi.org/10.1111/j.1467-8624.2004.00691.

Wellman, H. M., Fang, F., & Peterson, C. C. (2011). Sequential Progressions in a theory-of-mind scale: Longitudinal perspectives. *Child Development*, 82(3), 780–792. https://doi.org/10.1111/j.1467-8624.2011.01583.x.

Wellman, H. M., Fang, F., Liu, D., Zhu, L., & Liu, G. (2006). Scaling of theory-of-mind understandings in Chinese children. *Psychological Science*, 17(12), 1075–1081. https://doi.org/10.1111/j.1467-9280.2006.01830.x.

Wellman, H. M., Lopez-Duran, S., LaBounty, J., & Hamilton, B. (2008). Infant attention to intentional action predicts preschool Theory of Mind. *Developmental Psychology*, 44(2), 618–623. https://doi.org/10.1037/0012-1649.44.2.618.

Wellman, H. M., Phillips, A. T., Dunphy-Lelii, S., & LaLonde, N. (2004). Infant social attention predicts preschool social cognition. *Developmental Science*, 7(3), 283–288. https://doi.org/10.1111/j.1467-7687.2004.00347.x.

Wimmer, H., & Perner, J. (1983). Beliefs about beliefs: Representation and constraining function of wrong beliefs in young children's understanding of deception. *Cognition*, 13(1), 103–128. https://doi.org/10.1016/0010-0277(83)90004-5.

Woo, B. M., Chisholm, G. H., & Spelke, E. S. (2024). Do toddlers reason about other people's experiences of objects? A limit to early mental state reasoning. *Cognition*, 246, 105760. https://doi.org/10.1016/j.cognition.2024.105760.

Woodward, A. (1998). Infants selectively encode the goal object of an actor's reach. *Cognition*, 69(1), 1–34. https://doi.org/10.1016/S0010-0277(98)00058-4.

Yamaguchi, M., Kuhlmeier, V. A., Wynn, K., & VanMarle, K. (2009). Continuity in social cognition from infancy to childhood. *Developmental Science*, 12(5), 746–752. https://doi.org/10.1111/j.1467-7687.2008.00813.x.

Yeung, E. K. L., Apperly, I. A., & Devine, R. T. (2024). Measures of individual differences in adult Theory of Mind: A systematic review. *Neurosci Biobehav Rev.*, 157, 105481. https://doi.org/10.1016/j.neubiorev.2023.105481.

Youngblade, L. M., & Dunn, J. (1995). Individual differences in young children's pretend play with mother and sibling: Links to relationships and understanding of other people's feelings and beliefs. *Child Development*, 66(5), 1472–1492. https://doi.org/10.2307/1131658.

Yott, J., & Poulin-Dubois, D. (2012). Breaking the rules: Do infants have a true understanding of false belief? *British Journal of Developmental Psychology*, 30(1), 156–171. https://doi.org/10.1111/j.2044-835X.2011.02060.x.

Yu, C., Kovelman, I., & Wellman, H. M. (2021). How bilingualism informs Theory of Mind development. *Child Development Perspectives*, 15(3), 154–159. https://doi.org/10.1111/cdep.12412.

Yu, C.-L., & Wellman, H. M. (2023). Where do differences in Theory of Mind development come from? an agent-based model of social interaction and Theory of Mind. *Frontiers in Developmental Psychology*, 1, 1237033. https://doi.org/10.3389/fdpys.2023.1237033.

Yu, C. L., & Wellman, H. M. (2024). A meta-analysis of sequences in theory-of-mind understandings: Theory of mind scale findings across different cultural contexts. *Developmental Review*, 74, 101162. https://doi.org/10.1016/j.dr.2024.101162.

Zmyj, N., Prinz, W., & Daum, M. M. (2015). Eighteen-month-olds' memory interference and distraction in a modified A-not-B task is not associated with their anticipatory looking in a false-belief task. *Frontiers in Psychology*, 6, 857. https://doi.org/10.3389/fpsyg.2015.00857.

Cambridge Elements

Child Development

Marc H. Bornstein
National Institute of Child Health and Human Development, Bethesda
Institute for Fiscal Studies, London
UNICEF, New York City

Marc H. Bornstein is an Affiliate of the *Eunice Kennedy Shriver* National Institute of Child Health and Human Development, an International Research Fellow at the Institute for Fiscal Studies (London), and UNICEF Senior Advisor for Research for ECD Parenting Programmes. Bornstein is President Emeritus of the Society for Research in *Child Development*, Editor Emeritus of Child Development, and founding Editor of *Parenting: Science and Practice*.

About the Series

Child development is a lively and engaging, yet serious and real-world subject of scientific study that encompasses myriad theories, methods, substantive areas, and applied concerns. Cambridge Elements in Child Development addresses many contemporary topics in child development with unique, comprehensive, and state-of-the-art treatments of principal issues, primary currents of thinking, original perspectives, and empirical contributions to understanding early human development.

Cambridge Elements

Child Development

Elements in the Series

Autobiographical Memory and Narrative in Childhood
Robyn Fivush

Children and Climate Change
Ann V. Sanson, Karina Padilla Malca, Judith Van Hoorn and Susie Burke

Socialization and Socioemotional Development in Chinese Children
Xinyin Chen

Giftedness in Childhood
Robert J. Sternberg and Ophélie A. Desmet

The Adopted Child
David Brodzinsky and Jesus Palacios

Early Childhood and Digital Media
Rachel Barr, Heather Kirkorian, Sarah Coyne and Jenny Radesky

Equity for Children in the United States
Shantel Meek, Evandra Catherine, Xigrid Soto-Boykin and Darielle Blevins

Children's Defensive Mindset
Kenneth A. Dodge

Temperament and Child Development in Context
Liliana J. Lengua, Maria A. Gartstein, Qing Zhou, Craig R. Colder
and Debrielle T. Jacques

Life History and Child Development
Lei Chang and Hui Jing Lu

Stress in Childhood
Camelia E. Hostinar, Anna M. Parenteau, Geneva M. Jost, Sally Hang, Joanna
Y. Guan and Jamie M. Lawler

Theory of Mind in Childhood
Diane Poulin-Dubois

A full series listing is available at: www.cambridge.org/EICD

Printed by Integrated Books International,
United States of America